THE WINDING ROAD

THE WINDING ROAD

Criminal Courts, Civil Matters,
and the Ongoing Quest for
Access to Justice

Steven I. Platt

RAMSES HOUSE PUBLISHING LLC
BALTIMORE, MD

THE WINDING ROAD: Criminal Courts, Civil Matters, and the Ongoing Quest for Access to Justice
Copyright © 2023 The Platt Group Inc.

Published by Ramses House Publishing LLC, Baltimore, MD
www.publishingforlawyers.com

First Printing, 2023
ISBN 978-1-7351462-2-5 paperback; 10-digit: 1-7351462-2-6
ISBN 978-1-7351462-5-6 eBook

Notice: The book is written for attorneys, scholars, and laypeople who are interested in historical accounts, opinion, and analysis of economics, law, and politics on a local and federal level.

Library of Congress Control No.: 2022923059

Printed and bound in the United States of America

DISCLAIMER: The opinions expressed herein are solely the author's opinions and are based on his personal experience. The information contained in this book is provided for informational purposes only, and should not be construed as legal advice on any matter. The trans-mission and receipt of information, in whole or in part, via the Internet or through e-mail does not constitute or create a lawyer-client relationship.

The Platt Group Inc.
P.O. Box 6604
Annapolis, MD 21401

*With my deepest love, appreciation, and affection to
my expanded family; each of you has enriched
my life more than you will ever know
in your own unique ways.*

*To my son, Jason Benjamin Platt, and his wife, Anne
Fleetwood Platt; my daughter, Sarah Edan Carter, her
husband, Kevin Carter, and my cherished grandchildren, Dylan Emerson Carter, Benjamin Graham Platt,
and Charlie Robert Platt.*

*To my partner and "Significant Other" going on 20
years, Frances Hughes Glendening.*

*To my ex-wife, Patti Hartlove Platt, for the years she
partnered with me, raised our children, and gave me
the time to live these stories.*

*To the memory of my parents, Nathan and Adele Platt,
my grandfather, Charlie Platt, and my grandmother,
Rose Platt, whose voyage on stowage from Russia
to Ellis Island in 1913 laid the foundation for me to
live out their and my dreams.*

*My parents raised me to believe I could do anything
that I wanted, limited only by my own capabilities.
This book is the evidence that I believed them.*

THE WINDING ROAD
Criminal Courts, Civil Matters, and the Ongoing Quest for Access to Justice

PART ONE: CRIMINAL JUSTICE IN THE 21ST CENTURY

PART TWO: THE ROLE OF THE JUDGE IN INTERNATIONAL LAW

PART THREE: DISPUTE RESOLUTION AND ACCESS TO JUSTICE

Acknowledgments

I thank the persons who have made this possible by working with me to edit and print these blog posts and columns throughout the years and now to publish them in book form. They include my selfless, trusted, and dependable administrative assistant, Penny M. Simpson, and, of course, my publisher, Tatia Gordon-Troy, Esquire, and her publishing company, Ramses House Publishing, LLC.

I want to remember and thank the deceased friends and mentors who helped shape me and my career. The first mentor I'll mention is Maryland District Court Chief Judge Robert F. Sweeney, whose style, history, and career served as an inspiration and a role model for me. The second is Seventh Circuit Chief Judge Ernest A. Loveless, Jr. for whom I clerked and whose political, diplomatic, and interpersonal skills instructed my conduct for the rest of my life. The third is Court of Appeals Judge Howard S. Chasanow, and the fourth is Peter F. O'Malley, Esquire, who showed me through his example that honesty and integrity can be successfully reconciled with being an effective political and business operative.

I also thank for being my professional colleagues, now retired and good friends still: Judge Glenn T. Harrell, Jr.; Judge William B. Spellbring, Jr.; Judge C. Phillip Nichols, Jr.; Judge Larnzell Martin, Jr.; Judge Leo E. Green; Judge Theresa Nolan; Judge Paul Bowman; Judge Julia Weatherly; and William F. Edwards, Esquire.

About the Author

"It was not until 1973–75, however, that I was able to gain initial insights into what I already had observed: the intersection of politics and economics with the law."

My first stirring of interest in politics was when I was 15 years old and was confronted with the assassination of President John F. Kennedy. I reacted emotionally. I was in high school at a private military college preparatory school named Massanutten Military Academy, located in the heart of the Shenandoah Valley of Virginia in a little town named Woodstock, about 10 miles from my home of Strasburg, Virginia.

My family members were all Republicans. My grandfather had registered as a Republican, being convinced at the time that he owed allegiance to that party after emigrating from Russia and becoming a naturalized citizen during the then–Republican administration of President Theodore Roosevelt. My father, his only child, followed suit; and the women, my grandmother and later my mother, when they were allowed to register to vote, followed the patriarch of the family.

I, however, having been born on New Year's Day, January 1, 1947, and thereby a certified "Baby Boomer," with my childhood occurring during the 1950s and 1960s, I gravitated toward the vision, promise, philosophy, and style of the young, handsome President John F. Kennedy and the inspiration, a/k/a "Camelot," that he instilled in my generation. The differences of opinion on political issues and the resulting "discussions" at the dinner table with my family were, to say the least, interesting if not always enlightening.

From there, I read, listened, and thought about politics a lot, which led me to become involved in the political campaigns of John V. Lindsay for mayor of New York City, Robert F. Kennedy for U.S. Senate in New York in 1966 followed by his bid for president in 1968, and William Battle for governor of Virginia, all while I was a student at the University of Virginia in Charlottesville, majoring in, you guessed it: Government and Politics.

After a brief stint on active duty with the Maryland National Guard, I moved on to law school at The American University in Washington, D.C. I became further involved in my adopted state of Maryland's local politics, first in the management of a state and county political campaign (1970–71) and again in 1974 in Prince George's County, Maryland. I also served in Annapolis, Maryland, for two years (1971–73) as administrative-legislative assistant to then–state Senator Steny H. Hoyer, who has been a U.S. congressman since 1981 and currently serves as majority leader of The House of Representatives.

During those years, I got a good look at the profession and practices of politics at the federal, state, and local levels. That experience included managing and observing campaigns at every level and observing the practical effects of economics, power, and influence in politics.

It was not until 1973–75, however, that I was able to gain initial insights into what I already had observed: the intersection of politics and economics with the law. During this time is when I was fortunate enough to serve as law clerk to Prince George's County Circuit Court Chief Judge Ernest A. Loveless, Jr. of the Seventh Judicial Circuit of Maryland.

In 1976, I departed the comfort and security of the chamber of Chief Judge Loveless, Jr. to engage in law practice, including a stint as counsel to the Maryland Democratic Party, and chairmanship of the Prince George's County Human Relations Commission (1976–78). That was followed by my election to two four-year terms on The Orphans Court (Probate Court) for Prince George's County (1978–86).

In 1986, I was honored to be appointed by Governor Harry R. Hughes to serve on the Bench of The District Court of Maryland. I was further honored to be elevated to the Bench of The Circuit Court of Maryland by Governor William Donald Schaefer, where I served until 2007.

Finally, in 2007, I left the full-time Judicial Bench to enter the very different world of "alternative dispute resolution" or ADR. I also began my "Pursuit of Justice" blog during this period, and am still going strong to this day. The world of ADR has provided me with the opportunity to work in private dispute resolution system and design, conflict coaching, and consulting.

Such has been my personal and professional trajectory. These opinions represent the product of my journey to date. My limited hope, if not expectation, is that these opinions will motivate readers to examine their own opinions.

A 50-Year Addiction
with No Illusions

*"I do not suffer from any illusion that law, economics,
and politics are what matters to everyone,
or that they should."*

In 2014, I wrote an op/ed. for the *Capital Gazette* entitled, "Grand juries are an aging institution." Apparently, I caused quite a stir; I became sought-after by the likes of WMAR (ABC2) and WUSA9 (CBS), two local stations in the Baltimore/Washington, D.C. area. They not only wanted me to explain the grand jury process but, more importantly, to explicate my position on the use of grand juries and how I had come to the conclusions proffered in the article.

I penned the op/ed. a little more than three months after 18-year-old Michael Brown, Jr. had been fatally shot by police officer Darren Wilson, and about two days after the grand jury's findings were released to the public, setting off a litany of violent protests, looting, and fires across Ferguson, Missouri.

Upon hearing of the decision not to indict Officer Wilson, I castigated the grand jury process and questioned its utility, pointing to "the secrecy of its deliberations for months and the lack of accountability that has inevitably accompanied it" with the intent of raising serious questions about the aging institution:

> *The institution of the grand jury needs to be re-examined and restructured if we are to effectively ensure that the unique functions that it has historically performed continue to be carried on. This means that we must determine which of the functions that the grand jury now performs should be transferred to other offices or individuals that can perform them more efficiently, economically and with greater transparency.*

A holdover from the 14th century brought to these shores from Old England, the grand jury originated from a need to have people with "special knowledge of crimes in its neighborhood." Over time, the knowledge base of the grand jury declined. Even England saw fit to abolish it, when in 1933, it was finally decided that the grand jury had come to do badly what it had done well.

My op/ed. centered on whether the independence of the grand jury has been or can be preserved in practice as well as theory; whether the secrecy of the proceedings continues to serve the historic purposes for which it was developed, including the protection of the innocent; and whether the grand jury is presently equipped to handle a large volume of cases and still independently determine if probable cause exists to hold an accused for trial.

For quite some time, the grand jury has seldom exercised anything more than its routine power of approval or disapproval of those matters laid before it by our state's attorney. This is the principal reason why there is serious doubt as to whether the grand jury performs any useful duties today.

I evoke this particular opinion piece to prepare you for what you will find as you embark upon your reading journey. *The Winding Road: Criminal Courts, Civil Matters, and the Ongoing Quest for Access to Justice* is a compilation of my blog posts and newspaper columns written over the last 13 years or so in which I set out to both praise what's good and uncover what's bad about our criminal justice system, access to justice efforts, and the role of alternative dispute resolution systems and tactics in our system where politics, economics, and law intersect.

I do not suffer from any illusion that law, economics, and politics are what matters to everyone, or that they should. But I have been addicted to thinking, talking, and writing about them for over 50 years and have never tried to recover from that addiction. Other than my family, these are the things that have occupied my mind and directed my pen as a political activist, staffer, operator, lawyer, and judge on three different courts, and now as a private mediator, arbitrator, conflict coach, consultant, and op/ed. columnist and blogger.

Every article included in this book, long or short, was written and published under my self-proclaimed theme, *A Pursuit of Justice: The Intersection of Law, Economics, and Politics*. That "Pursuit" is still ongoing. The path memorialized in these pages, I believe, will lead readers to the intersection of law, economics, and politics where justice will be found, if it exists, perhaps partially obscured by signs reading "Under Construction–Slow Down."

The opinions remain largely untouched from when they were first published. These warts are all *unapologetically* mine. Hopefully, you will enjoy reading them and they will stimulate your own critical thinking on these subjects. I would like to think that my words can help rescue our relationships and institutions; if that is the result, my purpose will have been served.

As my father would tell me with some frequency, "You can learn from anybody." As I would find out in my life's journey, my father was wrong! You can learn from *almost* anybody, not all. Nevertheless, I recommend listening to everybody. You never know—you might learn something.

PART ONE

Criminal Justice in the 21st Century

Chapter 1

Criminal Justice System Reform

"[I]f we're going to conditionally release anyone, we should assess that person's risk of recidivating and flight ... rather than feed the current unfair and inefficient bail bond system."

The most valuable lesson I learned as a result of being lucky enough to have been appointed and elected to serve on three different Maryland courts, and being able to change my first name to "Judge," for more than 35 years was ironically not to judge people and situations too quickly.

I also learned that there is a lot of grey in this world, which should inform the level of certainty in the judgments we do make particularly when they affect the liberty and the quality of life of our fellow citizens.

That is true whether those judgments are in a courtroom, a legislative committee room or chamber, an executive office, or even on the street. Most of us human beings are more complicated than either our admirers or detractors would like to believe, or that we recognize.

For that reason, I have realized as a result of my experience that a great deal of humility, albeit not agonizing, should be a part of any judgments we do make both professionally and personally, particularly when those judgments are enforced by the power of the government.

These realizations have now dawned on enough opinion-makers and officials in all three branches of local, state, and federal government as well as academia to give rebirth to a wave of what the media is describing as "criminal justice reform."

"Criminal Justice Reform" is the subject matter and the agenda of the "Maryland Justice Reinvestment Coordinating Council," composed of diverse representatives of all three branches of Maryland government as well as academia. It has already sought guidance and expertise from a wide range of professional disciplines and recognized authorities on issues arising as a result of previous policies implemented far too quickly with, at best, inadequate or incomplete data to support them for essentially political and ideological reasons.

These ill-advised policies adopted in the 1980s, 1990s, and even the first decade of the 21st century resulted from politicians, policy-makers, and even some judges instinctively ignoring social scientists and their opinions in favor of politically popular positions designed to appeal to their constituents' prejudices and predilections.

Those prejudices and predilections resulted from earlier ideological and inadequately researched theories by social theorists and their political and cultural partisans on both the left and the right. These pseudo-scholars provided politically appealing but deceptively simple answers to complicated questions, including the influence of heredity and environment on the development of personalities. These profound questions deserved far more rigorous research as well as lengthier deliberation than what they got.

Examples of these almost hysterical theories, which drove criminal justice system policy for three decades, included the writings of John Dilulio, a conservative American academic predicting in the 1990s that "a new breed of super-predators, kids that have no respect for human life and no sense of the future, would terrorize Americans indefinitely."

This "analysis," in part, drove the legislation establishing "mandatory sentences." Fortunately, he turned out to be wrong and later retracted his demonstrably incorrect and unsubstantiated prediction in order to preserve the small quantum of credibility left to him even in academia.

Dilulio was certainly not alone on the "Right." Other "experts" as well as "Talking Heads" predicted crime would keep rising as a result of the decline of the traditional nuclear family and growing ethnic diversity even in the face of the dawning reality as the 21st century began that, in fact, crime was and remains today clearly on the wane in Maryland, in the United States, and around the world. This is undeniably occurring, notwithstanding pockets of resistance to that statistically documented trend in parts of certain urban and suburban centers, including our own Baltimore City.

The "Right" was clearly not alone in the finding that the social theories that they painstakingly formulated and espoused to explain the "rising crime rate" in the 1980s and 1990s were inapposite to comprehend the reality of reduced crime generally, as well as the greater safety of even many urban centers as the 21st century began and progressed.

The "wisdom" of many social theorists of the "Left" that crime could never be curbed unless inequality was reduced, and recently that the "Great Recession" would interrupt the downward trend of the crime rate, now look just as wrong and even as silly as the right wingers' theories that being brought up by one parent and playing a lot of computer games would unleash an unstoppable crime wave.

We retain in Maryland, however, at least the remnants of public policies developed to combat crime believed to have been caused by the factors explained above: (1) The "War on Drugs" with its mandatory sentences and severe sentences for non-violent drug offenses; (2) Pre-Trial Detention based on economic status and discredited punitive rationales; (3) the contested election of circuit court judges based on who can be toughest on crime; and (4) sentencing guidelines issued to encourage solely uniformity (*i.e.,* fairness based on the average or mean sentence of judges throughout the state).

These sentencing guidelines continue to be followed almost blithely by many judges, despite the fact that we know that the average or mean sentence isn't always the best sentence and often is not. Furthermore, they can be very inefficient, unfair, and costly.

We also know that our bail bond system is likewise very unfair, inefficient, and costly—both with respect to public safety and economically. This is an issue where, unlike a lot of other issues, the longer we think about it and observe the current system, the simpler and more apparent the proper method of addressing the issue becomes, thereby defying the conventional wisdom. Every effort to legislatively address this issue in the General Assembly has failed apparently because of the strength and campaign contributions of the bail bond industry. Each year, we simply return to the status quo.

The answer to this seeming inability to change an obviously unfair and inefficient system is simple. Convince Maryland's district and circuit court judges of the really obvious facts that requiring that violent offenders pay for and post a high cash surety or property bond won't make them any less violent or dangerous when they pay for it and return to the street. Nor will requiring a person with no history of violence or other indicia suggesting the risk of flight pay for and post a bond make them less likely to flee the jurisdiction before their trial or court date.

Empirically, we know that what will reduce the risk of further crime and/or flight is Pre-Trial Release Supervision. So, if we're going to conditionally release anyone, we should assess that person's risk of recidivating and flight and then provide for a level of supervision based on that assessment rather than feed the current unfair and inefficient bail bond system. If, in fact, they are dangerous, then they should not be released at all! In this way, we will proactively and effectively prohibit their further criminal behavior.

Maryland's district and circuit judges have the power to do that now. Legislation is not necessary to accomplish this. The education and orientation of Maryland's district and circuit court judges, as well as the encouragement of their chief and administrative judges to utilize the technology and human resources in the form of pre-trial release agencies and personnel in lieu of bail bonds, is all that is necessary. Judges have that discretion. They should exercise it.

This is clearly a time and an opportunity with historically unique bipartisan support and cooperation to substantially reform, in ways much needed and long overdue, the entire criminal justice system in Maryland. The Maryland Justice Reinvestment Coordinating Council is the vehicle to lead that effort. Let's hope that it does!

Chapter 2

Crime and Punishment in Maryland

"Some people see things as they are and ask 'Why?'
I see things as they never were and ask, 'Why Not?'"

As Governor-Elect Larry Hogan and Lt. Governor-Elect Boyd Rutherford ramp up their transition team operations with a goal of having "the top executives of the incoming Administration before they are sworn in," it would behoove them to pay attention, not only to the qualifications, but also the management style of the men and women who seek appointive office at the highest levels in the new government. It is particularly important in selecting those who will set policy and administer departments that impact the criminal justice system.

Crime, or law and order, etc., *i.e.*, the efficiency of the criminal justice system, generally is a difficult political issue. The issue is impossible to manage, let alone control. There are too many variables that drive the voters' perception of their level of personal safety and that of their community at any given moment.

Outgoing Governor Martin O'Malley brought the City-Stat Program that he implemented in Baltimore City to the state of Maryland, and properly got credit for it both electorally and in the media. Governor-Elect Larry Hogan said very little about criminal justice issues in the campaign. His focus was on economic and fiscal issues. But he will face criminal justice issues soon enough and whether he likes it or not, they will directly impact his ability to prioritize and address the urgent economic and fiscal issues confronting him.

With that in mind, the new governor has an opportunity to seize the moment and restructure the operations of the agencies of the executive branch that administer the criminal justice system so that they work more collaboratively. He also should reach out to the independently elected state's attorneys, county, and municipal officials to develop and then implement a comprehensive, efficient, and economical law enforcement strategy that is coordinated, transparent, and most importantly consistent, coherent, and understandable to law-abiding citizens and potential law-breakers, alike.

These policies would be developed through a new Criminal Justice Policy Group comprising the governor, lieutenant governor, the attorney general, comptroller, and appropriate cabinet secretaries, including the secretaries of Public Safety/Corrections, Parole & Probation, Juvenile Services, and Health, as well as the elected state's attorneys, and independently elected county and municipal officials and law enforcement officials, who control their respective police agencies. It would also include representatives of the legislature, who lead committees charged with the funding of law enforcement and prosecutors, as well as their oversight.

The judicial branch of government should participate in this effort; however, the judiciary can never be a partner in any law enforcement strategy because its role is to check and balance the legislative and executive branches of government.

Yet, judges of all courts should, where appropriate (*e.g.*, at the pretrial hearing on conditions of pre-trial release and sentencing hearings), be made aware of any existing law enforcement strategy that drives a prosecutor's decision to advocate for particular conditions of release and/or a sentence, or that result in a particular plea agreement being reached and presented to the court for binding approval.

The public does not divide between the branches of government the accountability for what they perceive to be the failures of the criminal justice system. On the contrary, they blame all branches of government, but particularly the judicial branch for the shortcomings of the system.

The citizens of Maryland expect the criminal justice system to confront the high rate of recidivism; the ever increasing cost of incarcerating offenders again and again to no avail; the lack of accountability of the system for the behavior of criminals repeatedly processed through the courts and the adult and juvenile correctional facilities; the lack of supervision of these offenders at times while they are incarcerated and certainly when they are returned to our communities; as well as the problem of witness and victim intimidation, including the threat of further violence to them when they cooperate with law enforcement and appear in court.

We will find out shortly whether all three branches of government are prepared to make a commitment to the collaboration and provision of additional resources, the funding to pay for them, and a very different approach to the treatment of charged and convicted criminal offenders within our criminal justice system.

The adoption of any new approach carries with it a significant political risk, particularly to those elected officials who must run every four years. The results of the implementation of any new system, including the one advocated in this space, even if successful, cannot be expected to be felt or even seen by the next election.

The risk, of course, is that if the judgment of those with responsibility and authority to make these decisions is to simply not make the effort because it is deemed to be too costly to establish economic interests who feed off the inefficiencies of the current system and are too risky politically to deal with now or in the immediate future, then expect more of the same failed policies and procedures we already have seen and the continued finger-pointing that has accompanied its documented failure.

In suggesting changes in the operation, structure, philosophy, policies, and procedures of our criminal justice system and in confronting those who cynically and comfortably predict that failure will ultimately and inevitably be the result of our officials trying to lead in a new direction, I cannot help but recall the words Robert F. Kennedy said about exercising political leadership:

> *Some people see things as they are and ask 'Why?' I see things as they never were and ask, 'Why Not?'*

Chapter 3

A 21st Century Criminal Justice System

"Who knows, it might even explain the irrational behavior of everyone from legislators to hardcore criminals."

Maryland's criminal justice system needs an unprecedented and thorough review. This column's purpose is to develop that theme and to suggest both further reasons to move that project forward and how to conduct an examination that will produce ideas, policies, and practices that can effectively and, most importantly, systematically address the 21st century challenges that lie ahead.

I witnessed as a lawyer participating in politics and then a judge without a partisan thought in my head, the 1980s, 1990s, and even the first decade of this 21st century produce at best a series of ad hoc executive judicial and legislative responses to some theoretical causes of crime—particularly urban crime.

The Economist magazine pointed out recently that John Dilulio, a conservative American academic, was predicting in the 1990s that "a new breed of super-predators, kids that have no respect for human life and no sense of the future," would terrorize Americans indefinitely.

Fortunately, he turned out to be wrong and was later required to retract his prediction in order to preserve a small quantum of credibility.

Dilulio was certainly not alone on the right. Other "experts" as well as "Talking Heads" predicted crime would keep rising as a result of the decline of the traditional nuclear family and growing ethnic diversity even in the face of the dawning reality as the 21st century began that, in fact, crime was and remains today clearly on the wane in Maryland, in the United States, and around the world. This is undeniably occurring notwithstanding pockets of resistance to that statistically documented trend in parts of certain urban and suburban centers.

The "wisdom" of many social theorists of the "Left" that crime could never be curbed unless inequality was reduced, and, recently, that the "Great Recession" would interrupt the downward trend of the crime rate, now look just as wrong and even as silly as the right wingers' theories that being brought up by one parent and playing a lot of computer games would unleash an unstoppable crime wave.

Why have our best social scientists on both the left and the right been so consistently wrong about what was happening and why it was happening in the field of criminal justice? Nicholas A. Christakis, a physician and sociologist at Yale University and co-director of the Yale Institute for Network Science, offers a plausible explanation.

In a nutshell, Dr. Christakis suggests that the social sciences have not kept pace with the natural science in "evolving with the times." Specifically, he cites "the perfection of cloning techniques giving rise to the field of stem cell biology, advances in computer science contributing to 'systems biology' as examples of a general trend toward the development of whole new fields of inquiry as well as university departments and majors resulting from fresh discoveries and novel tools in the natural sciences."

Contrast this with the social sciences that Dr. Christakis opines have "stagnated." In noticing the lack of creativity and innovation in the social sciences generally, Dr. Christakis points out that "they offer the same set of academic departments and disciplines that they have for nearly 100 years: sociology, economics, anthropology, psychology, and political science."

This culminates in politicians and policymakers instinctively ignoring social scientists and their opinions in favor of politically popular positions designed to appeal to their constituents' prejudices and predilections because social scientists' opinions are currently time-worn—and boring.

This results in a lack of confidence in and respect for these opinions. Examples include continuing to study monopoly power, racial profiling, and health inequality. We already know monopoly power distorts markets, people are racially biased, and illness is unequally distributed to social class. Repeatedly observing, studying, and talking about these well-established phenomena does not help to fix or change them.

Instead, Dr. Christakis urges, as do I, that social scientists "redeploy their time and resources to new fields such as social neuroscience, behavioral economics, evolutionary psychology, and social epigenetics. These disciplines are comparatively new and in some respects controversial. Not coincidentally, many lie at the intersection of the natural and social sciences.

These new interdisciplinary fields have the potential to provide answers to questions that heretofore have seemed inexplicable and to articulate areas of inquiry not yet discovered. For example, a better understanding of the structure and function of human social networks might help us to understand which individuals within social systems have an outsize impact on the spread of ideas and the governance of institutions, such as our correctional facilities.

It might even tell us how to avoid future takeovers of correctional facilities by gangs or maybe even how to break up or prevent the creation or maintenance of gangs in these facilities and elsewhere. Who knows, it might even explain the irrational behavior of everyone from legislators to hardcore criminals.

We already have seen in the last 25 years the results of the lack of forward movement in the social sciences. Politicians, policymakers, and even judges in all three branches of government, for essentially political reasons, have instinctively resorted to their own prescriptions for what they think their gerrymandered constituents believe ails the criminal justice system.

These arbitrary measures have included harsher prison sentences, particularly long mandatory sentences, the "War on Drugs," unnecessary racial profiling, "Stand Your Ground" statutes, potential invasions of privacy, and other measures that as time marches on are being shown to not only *not* effectively address the problems they supposedly were created to fix, but to be counterproductive by creating additional problems of their own.

It is, therefore, time for our best and brightest to use the cutting-edge social science tools and disciplines available to them, as this century unfolds, to systematically modernize our criminal justice system so that it can address the breadth and complexity of the problems that we face in the 21st century.

The best way to begin that process is through a joint initiative of the executive, legislative, and judicial branches of our state government, along with support from the Maryland State Bar Association, to empanel a select committee or commission to examine the future of the institutions and operations of the criminal justice system in Maryland.

Chapter 4

Judiciary's Role in Counterterrorism Must Be Defined

*"What is reasonable in light of the
21st century terrorist threat?"*

As the spring of 2013 unfolds, there are plenty of local, state, national, and international political and legal issues to occupy the interest of those of us who enjoy or are even addicted to reading and writing about them.

At the local level, we highlight county and city officials leaving office in disgrace after convictions resulting from appropriating public funds and human resources for corrupt illegal, illicit, and even prurient purposes.

At the state level, we observe our "Free State" finally abolishing the death penalty, dramatically expanding gambling, laying the foundation for a faster-than-a-snail's-pace transportation system in the future, wind energy farms, and a number-one–ranked educational system for all who are capable of contributing economically and culturally to our state.

Finally, nationally and internationally, we witness a newly elected and thereby emboldened President Barack Obama and a Republican party reflecting on the causes of its defeat and, at times, openly warring with itself ("wacko birds" vs. Old Guard) over national security and world-view issues.

This is brought about by a rapidly changing world caused by fast-paced globalization uncovering heretofore latent or repressed demands for freedom and communication, particularly by young people. These forces have been unleashed by the internet and its stepchildren, social media.

These phenomena are confronted with hostility, born of the moral outrage of religious fundamentalism, mostly Islamic, in the Middle East, Northern Africa, and parts of Southern Europe and Southeast Asia. This Islamic Fundamentalism frequently morphs into terrorist activity housed in cells, rebel armies, and militias, which know no national boundaries or allegiances.

In this context, we recently heard U.S. Senator Rand Paul (R. Ky.) filibustering for 13 hours the confirmation of President Obama's nomination of National Security Advisor John Brennan for CIA director. The pretext (I said "pretext" not "context") for the filibuster was the president's "Drone Policy." This policy was initially confused and complicated more than it needed to be by U.S. Attorney General Eric Holder's unnecessarily incomplete and incoherent answer to the seemingly very simple and purely hypothetical question posed by Senator Paul, to wit:

> *Does the President of the United States by himself have the authority to order the assassination of an American citizen on American soil if he is not at that moment an imminent threat to the national security of the U.S.?*

Belatedly, after a series of unclear and arguably evasive answers, Attorney General Holder finally answered, "No," to that question. Before that and probably to be fair even if the attorney general had answered clearly right away, we witnessed a dialogue that included advocacy of yet another "court," this one to provide a check and balance on the president's power to order drone strikes, in a manner similar to the work of a Foreign Intelligence Surveillance Act (FISA) Court when it reviews and authorizes electronic surveillance activities on our citizens.

Before the president proposes anything like that, he should implement the restructuring of the intelligence community mandated by the Intelligence Reform and Terrorism Prevention Act of 2004, although it has never effectively taken place.

Furthermore, in doing so, the role of the federal judiciary (if it has a role and responsibility for the supervision of our effort to combat terrorism) should be critically examined and clarified. To date, whether the federal judiciary has a role in supervising the combating of terrorism, on earth or in cyberspace, has never been clearly established or even systematically examined for the purpose of determining whether that court is an institution structured to play such a role and whether it is operationally capable of doing so.

The result is that 12 years after the 9/11 attacks and other breaches of national security (the last notorious one being in Benghazi, Libya, late last year), the institutional structure of U.S. counterterrorism appears to be at best incoherent and at worst incomprehensible. That should change and in implementing that change, President Obama should consider the ideas of his former colleague on the faculty of the University of Chicago Law School, Judge Richard Posner.

"Posner's book published in 2006, *Uncertain Shield: The U.S. Intelligence System in the Throes of Reform*, and also his book, *How Judges Think*, provide potentially important ideas for whoever is selected by Obama to conceptualize the restructuring of the U.S. Intelligence system and also the extent of the supervision of that system by the federal judiciary.

Judge Posner describes attempts to articulate the role and responsibility of the judiciary in combating terrorism, to date, including his own, as "incoherent" at best. The evidence to support that conclusion is abundant and convincing.

The judiciary currently has no court or official with overall judicial or even administrative responsibility for the review of counterterrorism. In fact, other than the judges assigned to the two Foreign Intelligence Surveillance Courts, federal judges do not even have security clearances. Most important, as Judge Posner points out, "federal judges have NO education, training or experience in national security matters" to inform or reference their decisions.

Clearly, at a time when courts are belatedly recognizing the value of specialized knowledge of the subject matter of their jurisdiction, to refer life and death issues perhaps on a massive scale to judges with no experience and no expertise in national security is ill-advised, dangerous, and fool-hardy.

The fact that the decisions of untrained federal district court judges would be subject to review by appellate judges and Supreme Court justices, also not chosen for their knowledge or training in national security, should provide little or no comfort. How the restructuring of our counterterrorism effort should proceed and what national or even international role the federal judiciary should have in its supervision are issues that will be critical for our country and the world.

The threshold issue to be decided is: What is reasonable in light of the 21st century terrorist threat?

The answer to that question depends on understanding the nature of the terrorist threat and the behavior of terrorists around the globe. That threat and the behavior of those who present it have never been studied and analyzed with a view toward determining what means of monitoring and addressing it are reasonable and can be explained if the goal is to prevent the attack.

We should put our best people on that a soon as possible! That would include constitutional scholars, writers, historians, as well as intelligence professionals, technologists, and retired Court of Special Appeals Judge Charles Moylan, who could sum it all up in 100 pages or less with historical insight and footnotes/references.

The Death Penalty Is Different, and It Should Be

*"[T]he evolving standards of human decency
will finally lead to the abolition of the death penalty
in this country."*

The responsibility for determining whether the death penalty should be imposed rests with you and you alone, and you must act with due regard for the consequences of your decision.

These words, if spoken in another context or with reference to any subject other than directing the taking of a human life by the government, might appear to belabor the obvious or to be unnecessarily or even obnoxiously condescending and pedantic. Somehow, however, when the U.S. Supreme Court admonishes a trial judge or a jury to this effect in a capital case, as it did in *Caldwell v. Mississippi*, it seems entirely appropriate and not insulting at all.

This is because "Death is Different."

A separate body of law both statutory and case-based (appellate judge-made law) has evolved as a result of litigation involving the death penalty in this state as well as in every state with a death penalty on the books and in the federal courts.

Almost all of it is constitutionally based in some way even if it involves interpretation of particular state statutes or rules of procedure.

In turn, this has caused trials as well as appeals in capital cases to be very different than they are in non-capital cases, including even other murder cases where there is no request for the death penalty. This is entirely appropriate.

Frequently heard in the halls of any courthouse is the term "due process," which I emphasize means "fundamental fairness." Capital cases, more than any others, raise the question in many different contexts of "how much process is due."

Clearly, more process is due in a case when the liberty of an individual is at stake as contrasted with a case where only his or her property is at risk. Even more process is due, however, to a person accused of a capital crime, when his or her very life is at issue. This issue of whether a defendant has received due process, *i.e.*, has he or she been treated fairly, is the subject of most appeals, including the appeal of the capital cases that I handled as a judge.

I will illustrate why both the trial and appeal in capital cases are different by discussing two of the issues raised on appeal in one of the capital cases that I handled.

I cannot ethically comment on the case with respect to any issues still pending. I am, however, free to discuss those issues that have already been decided and, for that reason, are a matter of public record and no longer issues in the case.

a. The Verdict Form

The first issue, and the more substantive one, resulted from the defendant being convicted of two separate first-degree murders as a result of his stabbing of an elderly couple to death after being confronted by them in their home, which he had broken into and entered moments earlier. The State requested the death penalty for both first-degree murders. The defendant chose a jury trial for both the guilt/innocence phase and the sentencing phase on both murder counts.

Prior to this case, the Rule of Procedure and the form promulgated by the Maryland Court of Appeals for the jury to report its verdict in a capital case as required by the death penalty statute simply did not provide for the situation in my case where there were two first-degree premeditated murders and the defendant was found guilty as a principal in the first degree of both.

The form simply provided for a single determination of the aggravating factors and mitigating factors. Therefore, it was necessary to modify the form or double it.

The more cautious approach, which I chose initially, was to simply submit two separate forms, one for each victim, so it would be clear that the jury made the required findings separately for each victim.

However, both the state's attorney and defense counsel recognized that under the particular facts of this case, the aggravating and mitigating factors associated with the murder of each victim would of necessity be the same. They, therefore, jointly requested a single form, which provided for the required separate findings on the issue of whether the defendant committed each murder as a "principal in the first degree" but integrated the other findings.

The state's attorney and defense counsel each had his own individual tactical reason for doing so, but their interests converged. Their agreement and the request for the single form were placed on the record. I then agreed to do what both sides had requested in lieu of the more cautious approach I had originally planned, which was to submit to the jury two completely separate forms.

The jury returned a verdict directing the imposition of a sentence of death for both murders, which I then imposed pursuant to the statute. That decision was by law automatically reviewed by the Maryland Court of Appeals. The defendant's new attorney on appeal, however, concluded that the defendant's trial attorney had made a mistake in requesting the integrated forms and that I had erred in approving it.

There is well-settled case law (judge-made law) that if you do not object to a judge doing something or not doing something that you cannot complain about it on appeal. It is called the law of "waiver" or "issue preservation."

In this case, not only was there no objection to the integrated form, there was a joint request for it. In this capital case, however, the Court of Appeals simply chose to *not* apply the procedural law on when an issue is waived and cannot be appealed. It did so by simply stating that it *did not wish* to dispose of the issue of whether the defendant had a constitutional due process right to have two separate determinations on separate forms of the aggravating and mitigating factors as to each death penalty requested. The Court of Appeals did so quite obviously because it felt that more process was due in a capital case than in any other. It then ruled that two separate forms must be used whenever more than one death penalty is requested in the same case.

Five of the seven judges of the court concluded that because I had used only a single form, they would affirm one death penalty sentence because it was clear that this was what the jury intended, but that the second death penalty sentence would be vacated.

One judge dissented and said that I had committed no error and even if there was error, it was waived and therefore both death penalty sentences should be affirmed.

Another judge dissented, saying both death penalty sentences should be vacated and the case returned to the trial court for resentencing.

By a majority vote of the judges of the Court of Appeals, this defendant remained one of the individuals on death row in Maryland. This ruling illustrates why death penalty cases are different.

b. Continuing Judicial Education

The other issue, which was less substantive but illustrates my point in a different way, arose because the defendant felt aggrieved that the chief judge of the Maryland Court of Appeals had directed prior to his case that in order for a circuit court judge to be assigned to preside over a capital case, he or she must have previously completed the Judicial Institute course, "The Handling of the Capital Case." The Judicial Institute is the organization that provides continuing judicial education for Maryland judges.

At the time I was assigned to the defendant's case, I was one of six judges on the Circuit Court for Prince George's County that had completed this course. The defendant's counsel's theory was that since registration for this course was completely voluntary, only a judge predisposed to favor the death penalty would enroll in and complete such a course. He then asserted that the defendant should not be required to have such a judge presiding over his case and that I should recuse myself for that reason.

The Maryland Court of Appeals, in ruling on the appeal of my denial of that motion, summarily rejected this theory. In doing so, it stated that because a judge educates him- or herself to be able to better handle capital or any other cases, such action cannot be considered proof or even evidence of any predisposition on the part of that judge to want to impose the death penalty; furthermore, this judicial education is to the benefit, not the detriment, of the parties—in the case, both the State of Maryland and the defendant.

The Court of Appeals firmly rejected the defendant's claim of a constitutional right to choose a judge of a particular philosophy beyond one that subscribes to his duty to apply the law fairly and impartially, as his oath requires.

What made this issue interesting for me instead of just silly is that defense counsel requested the right to *"voir dire"* (question) me on my attitude about the death penalty sentence in Maryland. I allowed him to do so, on the record, even though the Court of Appeals made it very clear in its opinion that I was not required to do so.

One of his questions was whether I personally thought there should be a death penalty sentence in Maryland. My answer was, "I don't know."

It seems to me that the central dilemma posed by this issue is that in order for the death penalty to serve as an effective deterrent, it must be swift and certain.

On the other hand, because it is the government taking of life from one of its citizens, not just his or her liberty or property, due process precludes both swiftness and certainty.

Therefore, the death penalty sentence is constitutionally precluded from effectively serving as a deterrent.

The only purpose behind the death penalty then is punishment, and a good argument can be made that the history of the death penalty, both in Maryland and elsewhere, is that this ultimate punishment has not historically been fairly and impartially imposed.

Indeed, retired and deceased Justice Harry Blackman reached this conclusion after many years as a pro–death-penalty U.S. Supreme Court Justice when he announced near the end of his judicial career that he would "no longer tinker with the machinery of death because it cannot be fixed."

Having already done so, I will do it again if the law requires it. I remain hopeful, however, that as the late Supreme Court Justice William J. Brennan, Jr., said, some day, not tomorrow, indeed perhaps years from now, "the evolving standards of human decency will finally lead to the abolition of the death penalty in this country."

Chapter 6

Post-Conviction: When All Else Has Failed

*"His services were sought by those who had
almost no hope for securing their freedom
or even their future survival."*

Have you ever had one of those *Kafka-esque* nightmares, or seen a movie where someone is convicted of a crime and sent to prison even though he or she didn't commit the crime? Well, some people, no doubt, have suffered that fate. Others, no doubt, think they have been wrongfully convicted of a crime whether they actually committed the crime or not.

These are clearly tragic cases where, because of an error by one of the lawyers, or even the judge, a jury convicts a person, who if not for that mistake, might have been found "not guilty." Some of these people may, in fact, actually have been innocent of the crime with which they were charged. As Henry Miller once wrote:

> *[T]o be a victim of one's own mistakes is bad enough, but to be a victim of the other fellow's mistake as well is too much.*

There is a forum in which such individuals can have their Petitions for Post-Conviction Relief heard. I will describe that process and will memorialize one of the premier practitioners of that specialized area of the law, Fred Warren Bennett.

Post-Conviction Relief is a form of legal recourse available to persons who believe they have been convicted of a crime due to an error by one of the participants in the trial.

There are numerous types of allegations that a petitioner may assert in the Petition for Post-Conviction Relief. These include claims of misconduct or serious error by the prosecutor or the trial judge, a tainted jury, or a constitutionally or legally defective sentence. These allegations must not have been previously adjudicated or subject to adjudication at the trial or on appeal.

Of all the possible allegations, "ineffective assistance of trial defense counsel" is the most common. To better understand how an issue, which would give rise to a request for Post-Conviction Relief could develop, take the following hypothetical example:

Last year, Clare allegedly broke into Kimberly and Sam's house. While in the house, Clare stuffed her book-bag full of poetry books, which, considering the rising cost of fine verse, were collectively valued at $500. Soon after, the police apprehended Clare.

At her trial, she was found guilty of Theft over $500 and Second-Degree Burglary. She was sentenced to 15 years in prison. While 15 years would give her ample time to read the prison's poetry collection, after three months in jail, Clare had other plans and obtained a lawyer, Public Defender Louis.

On behalf of Clare, Louis filed a Petition for Post-Conviction Relief alleging that the previous Public Defender, Matt, was ineffective at trial and that if he had been effective, Clare would not have been found guilty.

In her Petition for Post-Conviction Relief, Clare alleged three reasons why Matt was ineffective at trial:

- *First*: Matt failed to object to hearsay statements being offered by one of the State's witnesses (Reasonable Competence);

- *Second*: Matt was appointed to represent Clare only three days before the trial and therefore had time for only one conversation with Clare regarding the case (Sixth Amendment Right to Counsel);

- *Third*: In a criminal case four years ago, Matt successfully defended Kimberly and Sam (Presumption of Prejudice).

In order to sustain any or all of these allegations, Petitioner Clare, will have the burden, at her Post-Conviction hearing, of proving that she was deprived of the effective assistance of counsel, and that, were it not for the deficiencies of her trial counsel's performance, she would have been found "not guilty."

a. Reasonable Competence

Clare is going to face the most difficult time proving her first allegation. A lawyer does not have to perform perfectly at trial in his or her representation of a client. The lawyer has to act "as a reasonably competent attorney would have acted" considering the circumstances of the case. In order to prove that Matt's failure to object caused his representation to be ineffective, Clare would need to prove that the outcome of the trial would have been different if Matt had acted "as a reasonably competent attorney would have acted" considering the circumstances. This is not easy to prove for two reasons:

- *First*, when looking at the context in which his failure to object occurred, it may have been reasonable for him not to object, either because the testimony offered by the State's witness was only potentially hearsay and not clearly so (a "gray area"), or previous Defense counsel could have reasonably refrained from objecting for "tactical reasons." If either of these explanations of previous defense counsel's action or inaction were believed by the Post-Conviction Court, then Post-Conviction Relief would not be available to Clare.

  If the Post-Conviction court can't conclude that the statement was definitely hearsay and/or that the action of Defense counsel was not "tactical," then the Post-Conviction Court certainly could not conclude that the outcome of the trial would have been different had Matt objected. Therefore, it could not grant Post-Conviction Relief and the verdict of the trial court would stand.

- *Second*, even if Matt should have objected and/or the hearsay statement should not have been allowed, Clare would still have to convince the Post-Conviction Court that the hearsay statement was so important that had it not been uttered, she would have been found not guilty. Appellate courts of this State have ruled that there is a strong presumption that the trial counsel is effective and that these decisions are tactical and are not to be judicially second-guessed by a subsequent court.

b. Right to Counsel

Clare is more likely to succeed on her second claim. Because Matt was not appointed as Public Defender until a few days before trial, Clare may be able to make a strong argument that she was not accorded her Sixth Amendment Right to Counsel. The Sixth Amendment of the U.S. Constitution guarantees assistance of counsel in criminal cases, such as the one being described in this example. However, merely having a lawyer show up for the trial does not fulfill this duty of assistance of counsel.

If Clare can convince the court that Matt was unprepared for trial because he didn't have time to learn the facts of the case, that he did not effectively question and prepare witnesses for that reason, and that because he only spoke briefly with Clare before the trial, making Matt's performance otherwise ineffective, then Clare may prevail. A trial counsel's performance is "ineffective" if it falls below the standard required by the court, which was set forth in the Maryland case, *Strickland v. State*.

c. Presumption of Prejudice

Clare's best chance of having the trial overturned is with her third allegation. Because Matt had previously represented the victims, Kimberly and Sam, and at the trial he was called upon to examine them, there is potentially a conflict of interest and a presumption of prejudice. Before the trial, Matt should have informed his client and the court of this potential conflict in his interest; because he did not do so, if the presumptive conflict can be shown to have affected his conduct at Clare's trial and that the verdict was also affected, Post-Conviction Relief in the form of a new trial may be required.

If the Post-Conviction Court decides that one or more of Clare's allegations has merit, the court has the authority to grant various types of relief. The court can vacate the conviction and sentence, order a new trial, grant a re-sentencing, and order other forms of specific relief depending on the nature of the error committed.

While it is true that the error of one moment can become the sorrow of a whole life, with Post-Conviction Relief, the error can be corrected and the sorrow avoided for the wrongfully accused. It is also true, however, that post-trial second-guessing and finger-pointing are easy to start, but quite difficult to successfully pursue—and properly so.

Certainly one of the preeminent practitioners of Post-Conviction Law, and an architect of some of it in this state, was tragically taken from us as a result of an automobile accident this past week. Fred Warren Bennett, affectionately referred to by some of his friends on the Bench and in the Bar as "The Cold Case Lawyer," was dedicated to his clients in a way that far exceeded most professional attorney-client relationships. His services were sought by those who had almost no hope for securing their freedom or even their future survival—and in some cases deservedly so.

When Fred Warren Bennett agreed to represent a client no matter what that client had done, no matter what public opinion had been formed about him or her or what they did, Fred fought for them. He prepared and prepared! Prosecutors knew they had to be as thorough as Fred in their research and presentations.

Fellow lawyers in the Criminal Defense Bar felt his zeal and his judgment of them, many times in their eyes unfairly, as he argued vehemently for relief for his client based on what he considered the lawyer's deficient performance and representation of the client's interests in prior proceedings.

Agree with him or not, in a professional world not sought-after by many, Fred Warren Bennett excelled and he will not be forgotten by those of us who observed his caring and competent advocacy on behalf of clients who had no other advocate or friend in this world.

Chapter 7

Explanation for Violence at Virginia Tech Provided by Shakespeare

"I have yet to see a serious act of violence ... provoked by ... feeling shamed and humiliated ... that did not represent the attempt to ... undo this loss of face."

As I sat in my regular seat at Washington, D.C.'s Shakespeare Theater less than a week after Seng Hui Cho's shooting rampage at Virginia Polytechnic Institute left 33 people dead including the shooter, I watched the play, *Titus Andronicus*, labeled by "Literary Associate" Akiva Fox in the Playbill Program as "Shakespeare's most violent play." As it unfolded, I couldn't help but reflect on what makes the violence in Titus Andronicus more pronounced and therefore more unsettling than the other Shakespeare plays I have seen performed on that same stage.

The answer is that unlike the other plays I have seen, the results of the violence in this one are not only graphic but the audience cannot avoid seeing them unless it collectively looks away from the stage. Furthermore, in this production unlike some others, there is no attempt to soften the visual trauma called for in the original script by employing tongue-in-cheek humor or the stylization of the violence so often used to soften the discomfort it might otherwise produce.

So, too, it is with the slaughter at Virginia Polytechnic Institute and before that at Columbine High School. We watched them on television and we saw pictures in the print media. There has been very little attempt to shield the victim's family, friends, colleagues, and the public generally from the modern-day equivalent of the fictional severed heads, hands, and tongues exhibited on stage in *Titus Andronicus*.

The result is that we are again witnessing the usual response from government at all levels. Virginia Polytechnic Institute is investigating, the state of Virginia is investigating, and the federal government is investigating. Each has established its own distinguished and well-intentioned panel and taskforce, each expertly staffed with well-credentialed psychiatrists, psychologists, and law enforcement officials to determine "what happened," "the facts," and the "root causes" of the behavior that caused the tragic deaths of 32 innocent people and serious injuries to others in what had been a bucolic campus in rural Virginia.

Let's suppose they do just that. Obviously, that would mean that one or more of these investigations will somehow find a way to diagnose *ex post facto* the depression, psychosis, and/or other mental condition that presumably developed to the point of driving Seng Hui Cho's homicidal rage and actions.

What then?

Even if we believe that the pronounced diagnosis is not just a theory, but a convincing one, as University of Virginia Sociology professor Donald Black points out:

> [I]t cannot explain why many other people with those same conditions or diseases, in fact the vast majority of people with those conditions, have never done and will never do what Cho did.

So what use would this information or "profile" be to society or to government? Are we prepared to take steps as a part of the college admission process to require the testing necessary to profile and then screen applicants and even current students attending our colleges and high schools?

Then are we prepared to exclude or even suspend or expel those who fit the profiles? Will we let them back in if they consent to therapy? Who will monitor and ultimately certify that an applicant can be accepted or a student has been "treated" sufficiently to merit readmission to classes and living quarters at a college, university, or a high school in our county, state, and nation? Who will pay for all of this?

As a practical matter, the answer to all of these questions is that none of these procedures can be put into place in a manner that would be workable and affordable. Therefore, applying a cost-benefit analysis, it is clear that it is not efficient to even contemplate it.

Moreover, even if we were prepared to pay for the diagnostic personnel and procedures to be employed, we could not effectively shield our citizens from potential harm without victimizing a large population whose only sin is needing mental health treatment, and an even larger population whose privacy has to be wholesale invaded solely because they applied to college or wanted to attend high school.

What then can we do? We can recognize that the risk of a repetition of the behavior we just endured at Virginia Polytechnic Institute cannot be entirely eliminated by determining what psychological conditions and/or psychiatric disorders Cho, or any other particular individual, was suffering from at the time of his deadly rampage and then trying to detect its presence in the general population by massive testing.

We can also recognize that Professor Donald Black's theory that "[m]ost violence is a way that people handle grievances" is worth considering and researching further because there is empirical evidence to support it.

If you assess the likelihood that a particular individual will commit a violent act, do not examine his upbringing or his mental condition. Look at his relationship with the group that constitutes his potential target, *e.g.,* students at university, dorm residents, student organizations, faculty, etc. If it is noticeably troubled, take precautions.

This actually is doable with existing professionals and paraprofessionals (student and faculty counselors, if they are organized and trained to observe and monitor these situations and individuals). As James Gilligan, a scholar of violence who was also a prison psychiatrist, has written:

> *I have yet to see a serious act of violence that was not provoked by the experience of feeling shamed and humiliated and that did not represent the attempt to prevent or undo this loss of face.*

Professor Black further develops this theory by emphasizing:

> *[T]he vectors of social geometry propel individuals to do what they do ... There are particular social configurations that produce various kinds of behavior. It is the configuration that generates the violence. It is not peculiar to the individual. There is not something in the individual's mind that brings the event into existence.*

Based on my own experience of observing evidence of criminal activity for 25 years on the Bench, I don't agree completely with Professor Black that "there is not something in the individual's mind" that motivates criminal activity. As a minimum, my experience tells me that an individual's personality, shaped by his or her biology, environment, and history, may influence a response to a particular social configuration or relationship. But the theory is still worth researching further and developing for the reasons cited earlier.

This theory of Professor Black's, even if it is not accepted in its pure form, still threatens some bedrock premises of our criminal justice system. The theory, as *Washington Post* columnist Shankar Vedantam notes:

> *... threatens conservative beliefs about the role of personal responsibility and accountability for criminal acts as well as lib-*

eral notions about there being a psychological or 'humanistic'
explanation for all behavior.

As long as no one claims to know how to predict future behavior and therefore how to stop human beings from killing or hurting other human beings, we ought to explore every possible explanation for what people do and why they do it.

The debate about what we do about violent crime should not be limited to what columnist E.J. Dionne, Jr. calls "technical details or ideological predispositions."

More on another day.

Chapter 8

Exclusionary Rule: To Be or Not to Be? That Is No Longer the Question

*"It is the "price' our society pays for enjoying
the freedom and privacy safeguarded by
the Fourth Amendment."*

A number of years ago, I had the pleasure of joining a distinguished prosecutor, now Montgomery County Deputy State's Attorney John Maloney, and a preeminent defense attorney, Louis J. Martucci, in a discussion of the wisdom of maintaining what is known as the "Exclusionary Rule." That rule requires a trial court judge and, ultimately perhaps a majority of whatever panel or appellate court considers the issue, to exclude any evidence obtained by a law enforcement officer in a manner in which, in the opinion of the court, was in violation of the Fourth, Fifth, or Sixth Amendments to the U.S. Constitution.

In his part of the exchange, billed dramatically as "What Is an Officer to Do?" Prosecutor Maloney bemoaned a then-recent decision of the Maryland Court of Appeals, which limited the right of a police officer to detain a citizen for "investigation" even if the citizen "consents" to remain with the officer.

While defense attorney Martucci celebrated this same decision, Maloney pointed out that the decision came after three years, during which "different lawyers and judges have been in comfort-controlled courtrooms debating Trooper Smith's actions." Maloney then quite appropriately noted:

> *Trooper Smith had a few seconds to decide on the side of the road in the early morning hours what to do. If those judges, in over three years, cannot agree on what was proper, how is the officer supposed to know in a few seconds?*

My answer, as a judge, is that it is clear that this officer could not have known at the time that he could not constitutionally detain for further "investigation" one Peter Michael Ferris who was driving 92 miles an hour at 1:06 am on Route 70 in Washington County, Maryland, just because he noticed that Ferris had bloodshot eyes and was "acting fidgety and nervous," even if Ferris said he "didn't mind" in response to the trooper's asking whether he would mind stepping to the back of his vehicle to answer some questions.

It is equally clear now, however, that in the future, the officer will know. The cost of his learning is that the truth about Peter Michael Ferris being in possession with the intent to distribute drugs was ultimately excluded from evidence and the prosecution of this particular criminal was crippled.

There are essentially three schools of legal opinion on the use of this judicially created legal remedy to exclude otherwise truthful and reliable evidence in a criminal trial:

- The first is, it should never be done.

- The second is, it should be utilized only on a limited basis after the application of a judicial cost-benefit analysis.

- The third is, it should be invoked at any time evidence is seized in violation of a defendant's constitutional rights.

The Exclusionary Rule has been applied in federal prosecutions since 1914. It has applied to state criminal trials since 1961. Since those dates, it is fair to say that the view that this doctrine, created to regulate police conduct, should be abolished has never gained acceptance by the judiciary of any state or the federal courts.

As a result of its acceptance, albeit perhaps not enthusiastically in some quarters, the Exclusionary Rule in one form or another appears to be embedded firmly in the law.

The proper scope of the rule remains very much at issue. To illustrate the debate, contrast the opinions of former U.S. Supreme Court Justices Byron White and William Brennan.

In 1984, Justice White in two opinions, flat out stated that,

> *[T]he exclusionary rule was not part of the Fourth Amendment, but was a remedy created by the courts solely to deter police violations of the amendment. Whether to apply the rule in a given case depends on a cost-benefit analysis.*

In those same cases, Justice Brennan dissented, stating that the rule "was part of the Fourth Amendment and that the admission of evidence was as much of a violation as its initial seizure." Brennan went on to acknowledge that,

> *[T]his restriction on official power means that some incriminating evidence will go undetected if the government obeys these constitutional restraints. It is the "price' our society pays for enjoying the freedom and privacy safeguarded by the Fourth Amendment.*

Are you, as a citizen, willing to pay that price? Defense attorney Louis Martucci says you, as a citizen and motorist, should be pleased and your confidence restored that Maryland's Court of Appeals' judges are willing to closely scrutinize police conduct in suggesting "consent searches" and ready to exclude evidence if it is obtained in a manner that does not withstand that scrutiny.

Prosecutor John Maloney says:

> *Law enforcement is dangerous enough without putting these impossible burdens on the officers and troopers.*

He also expresses hope that his young daughter, Maggie Maloney, "when she is Supreme Court Justice, will write an opinion to overturn this case."

As a trial court judge, I took an oath to apply the law, which includes opinions from the Maryland Court of Appeals. So, I will, at least for the time being, more closely scrutinize consent searches that follow traffic stops even though I find Judge Howard Chasanow's dissent more persuasive than the majority opinion in this case.

I will patiently await, however, the opinion of Justice Maggie Maloney, citing Maryland Judge Chasanow's dissent for further and perhaps more enlightened guidance and direction.

PART TWO

The Role of the Judge in International Law

Chapter 9

Judges and National Security: The Supervision of Counterterrorism

*"[F]ederal judges have no education or experience
in national security matters."*

Last week, I attended the Fourth Annual Meeting of the American College of Business Court Judges in Chicago, along with several other judges from our state who preside over dockets assigned to the Business and Technology Case Management Program in the Maryland circuit courts.

At that conference, the keynote speaker was Judge Richard A. Posner, who is a federal circuit judge as well as a senior lecturer at the University of Chicago Law School. Although Judge Posner, on that occasion, spoke on a topic not of general interest to anyone except the judges present for our meeting and perhaps not even to all of them, he did discuss a wide range of subjects during informal discussions that preceded his formal remarks.

So that my bias is fully disclosed, I consider Judge Posner to be the finest mind and, because of that, the most interesting judge and legal writer that this country has produced in the last quarter of a century.

He has written books and articles on a wide range of subjects that include but are not limited to law and economics, psychology, national security issues, and even a book entitled, *Sex and Reason.*

That he has never been nominated for the U.S. Supreme Court is unfortunately more of a comment on the potential political controversy, which could no doubt be generated by a sensationalist focus on his extensive paper trail than on his qualifications for the highest court.

The 56 books and articles written by Judge Posner contain some discussions of unconventional even provocative subjects. That fact coupled with the intensely politicized theatrics that have come to characterize the confirmation process that any nominee of either party must undergo if nominated for the federal bench, and particularly the Supreme Court, has probably deterred presidents of both parties from nominating him for the Supreme Court and perhaps even deterred him from seeking the job.

As President-Elect Barack Obama, literally working across town in the same city we were meeting in—Chicago—focuses on the selection of his "national security team," he might want to consider the ideas of his former colleague on the faculty of the University of Chicago Law School, Judge Posner. Posner's book published in 2006, *Uncertain Shield: The U.S. Intelligence System in the Throes of Reform,* and also his most recent book, *How Judges Think,* provide potentially important ideas for whomever is selected by Barack Obama to conceptualize the restructuring not only of the U.S. Intelligence System, but also the extent of the supervision of that system by the federal judiciary.

The restructuring of the intelligence community is mandated by the Intelligence Reform and Terrorism Prevention Act of 2004. That restructuring has never effectively taken place. Posner further points out that the role of the judiciary to combat terrorism, or whether it has a role and responsibility for the supervision of our effort, has never been clearly established.

The result of this is that seven years after the 9/11 attacks, the institutional structure of U.S. counterterrorism is in disarray. The Department of Homeland Security is at best a work in progress and that progress is almost universally acknowledged to be as Posner describes it, "slow and painful."

The role and responsibility of the judiciary in combating terrorism is described accurately by Posner as "incoherent" at best. The evidence to support both of those conclusions cited by Judge Posner is both abundant and convincing. The judiciary currently has no court or official(s) with overall judicial or even administrative responsibility for the review of counterterrorism. In fact, other than the judges now assigned to the two foreign intelligence courts, federal judges do not even have security clearances.

Judge Posner points out that "federal judges have no education or experience in national security matters" to reference their decisions. Other points Judge Posner makes are that "the criminal justice system is designed for dealing with ordinary crimes, not global terrorism as illustrated by the rules that entitle a person arrested to a prompt probable cause hearing before a judge and that criminal trials be generally open to the public except in certain limited circumstances."

The Supreme Court already has invalidated the original version of the Military Commissions that the Bush administration's Defense Department attempted to establish to try captive "terrorists" before they even have a trial. Of greater concern to Judge Posner is what he describes as the "strangeness" of allowing a federal district court judge in Detroit, Michigan—randomly selected from 700 federal judges with no knowledge or experience in national security—to decide "as momentous an issue as whether the National Security Agency's conduct of electronic surveillance outside the boundaries of the Foreign Intelligence Surveillance Act was illegal. She decided that it was.

The one court, the Foreign Intelligence Surveillance Court, with judges who have at least some self-taught expertise and the security clearances to go with it, was bypassed because its jurisdiction was limited to foreign intelligence surveillance warrants.

The National Security Agency program under attack in the litigation involved warrantless surveillance, thereby giving new dimension to the elevation of form over substance.

The fact that this untrained federal district court judge's decision, as well as other untrained federal district court judges' decisions, is subject to review by judges on appellate courts and the Supreme Court—who also are not chosen for their knowledge or training in national security—provides little or no comfort to Judge Posner.

How the restructuring of our counterterrorism effort should proceed and what national or even international role the judiciary should have in the supervision of it are issues, the resolution of which will be critical for our country and the world.

Chapter 10

Dubai: A City of Contrasts

"The ruling classes of Emirati are quite proud of their city, its beauty, and their wealth ..."

From April 19, 2012, through April 29, 2012, Retired North Carolina Special Superior Court Chief Judge Ben F. Tennille (Business Court) and I had the honor and very interesting experience of traveling to Dubai, the commercial capital city of the United Arab Emirates (UAE), to "consult" with selected members of the Iraqi judiciary on subjects related to the administration of "Business Courts" and the management of "Business Litigation" in Iraq.

Dubai was chosen by us for both personal and professional reasons, which I will explain below. Suffice to say, I told Judge Tennille that if the representatives of the U.S. Department of Commerce and the State Department with whom we were working wanted to know why we were firm in our position that Dubai was the ideal venue for our "consultation" as opposed to Baghdad and as it turns out Cairo, tell them:

> *Judge Platt still thinks that there are weapons of mass destruction near Baghdad and he further believes that particularly in light of his ethnic and religious heritage that we should avoid at*

all costs even the appearance of involvement in the current Egyptian elections and the 'Arab Spring' generally.

These two pre-textual positions worked and we were dispatched to Dubai.

Dubai is a city of contrasts, which are immediately noticeable. Forty-five years ago, Dubai was a fishing village. Today, it has more skyscrapers than Manhattan, including the tallest building in the world. Unfortunately, many of these commercial and mixed-use buildings stand in various states of incomplete construction, which has been interrupted by the worldwide recession; 25 percent of the cranes in the world are located in Dubai and are being utilized in the construction of these buildings whose architecture can best be described as "futuristic."

However, many of these cranes are at a standstill, awaiting a fresh infusion of investor capital liberated from the throes of the global recession in order to finish the construction of the city they were placed there to help create. There are signs that economic relief is on the way.

The ruling classes of Emirati are quite proud of their city, its beauty, and their wealth, which is on ostentatious display in selected parts of the cities of Dubai and Abu Dhabi, the political capital city. One of their "malls," which makes our malls look like strip shopping centers, contains a ski resort that is full size with real snow brought in. You can watch the skiers from a restaurant in the mall. There are also numerous waterfalls, huge fountains, and other water-inspired displays throughout the malls, as well as the city itself, which is in a desert irrigated for both functionality and aesthetic effect.

Those displays of beauty and wealth are not located in the neighborhoods, which house the laborers whose hard work and sweat built the more impressive commercial and tourist zones of the City of Dubai and still provide the labor that keeps the city pristine and functional.

These neighborhoods largely still resemble the fishing village Dubai used to be. The residences and commercial establishments and structures appear to be in their original state and are best described as humble (residences) and honky-tonk (commercial). The contrast with the financial and commercial sections of the city is glaring.

All of this having been noticed, the appearance and role of women in Dubai, the United Arab Emirates, Iraq, and most of the Middle East provides by far the starkest contrasts, especially to the untrained eyes and the minds of those of us comparatively unschooled in the religious doctrinal and cultural dictates of traditional and modern Islam.

Judge Tennille and I were boarded at The Ritz Carlton Hotel, a five-star hotel located in the Financial Centre of Dubai. In the lobby and restaurants of that hotel and other similar venues, approximately 50 percent of the women were cloaked in *burqas* and veiled so that only their eyes were visible. The other 50 percent wore clothing that would not be noticeable at all in a hotel lobby or a shopping center in the United States. Only in the bars were there no *burqas*.

The 21 Iraqi judges whom we were there to "consult" with were all men. Women cannot be judges in Baghdad. They can be "Public Prosecutors." One "Public Prosecutor" accompanied the 21 Iraqi judges. She was allowed to participate fully in our program, including those parts where we sought to be interactive. In fact, she contributed very positively to the program without appearing to be inhibited in doing so at all.

For this, in my mind, she deserves a great deal of credit because, notwithstanding the fact that her Islamic faith and that of the judges she accompanied allowed her to fully participate professionally, including asking questions and commenting on our discussions, she was not allowed, in any way, to socialize or talk with her male colleagues nor with Judge Tennille and me during breaks in the program and during meals.

This translated visually and audibly into coffee breaks where she would walk into the room and sit at a table, which would result in everyone else heading to other tables. It resulted in her sitting alone or at one end of a long table for meals while the men gathered at a separate table or at the opposite end of a large table.

Judge Tennille and I were specifically oriented that we should not, for diplomatic reasons, attempt to, in any way, physically contact this or any woman, including shaking her hand, nor should we attempt to engage in any conversation with this or any Muslim woman except in a purely professional programmatic context.

In the face of these two worlds of commercial affluence, even opulence and traditional Islam co-exist (sometimes, I gather, uneasily), Judge Tennille and I, through the good offices of the U.S. Department of Commerce working with the State Department, were transported to Dubai to consult with the Iraqi judiciary on the role that "Business Courts" can play in providing the stability of laws and institutions necessary to compete effectively for foreign investment.

In so doing, the issues we faced, in some ways, bore a remarkable resemblance to the issues faced in the United States when specialized business courts were proposed in many of the states, including Maryland.

Chapter 11

The Hague Works for Peace, Security, and Justice Across the Globe

"[I]f we were capable of taking in all the suffering of all those people, we would not be able to live."

For one week this past September 2008, I and one other Maryland Judge, Cathy Hollenberg Serrette, by coincidence also from the Circuit Court for Prince George's County, had the honor and the pleasure of participating in the Fourth Sir Richard May Seminar on International Law and International Courts with a group of other judges from around this country and South America.

This seminar was conducted at The Hague, Netherlands, a unique and captivating city known at times as a "Special City" or "The Hague as Judicial Capital of the World." However, the most accurate and the most recent description that best comports with the indelible impression that I and other participants came away with after our whirlwind learning experience for the six days we were there is, "The City of Peace, Security and Justice."

The seminar was sponsored by the International Judicial Academy (IJA), which is a nonprofit educational institution chartered in the

District of Columbia in 1998. Its stated mission is to provide high-quality education programs for judges, court administrators, and other legal professionals from countries around the world so they can "function in a modern, fair, efficient, accessible, and transparent court system."

Other sponsors were the JEHT Foundation, The American Society of International Law, and the Atlantic and Pacific Exchange Program. JEHT stands for the core values that underlie the Foundation's mission: Justice, Equality, Human Dignity, and Tolerance. It seeks to "expand the constructive role that the U.S. can play in promoting international justice, human rights and the rule of law at home and abroad."

The American Society of International Law founded in 1906 and chartered by Congress in 1950 "fosters the study of international law and promotes the establishment and maintenance of international relations on the basis of law and justice."

Finally, The Atlantic and Pacific Exchange Program is a Dutch-American nonprofit organization that organizes high-level international study programs for senior– and mid-level government officials, business executives, journalists, and academics. It consists of two jointly operating foundations, one headquartered in Rotterdam, The Netherlands, and the other located in Washington, D.C. The Program does not attempt to sell any political philosophy or idea; it is completely neutral in this regard.

The experience that this distinguished group of sponsors put together for us was intense and ran from 8:30 am to at least 5:00 pm on all but one day. We visited almost every international tribunal and organization and the beautiful and functional buildings that house them in The Hague. They included the International Court of Justice located in the Peace Palace; The Hague Conference on Private International Law; The Special Court for Sierra Leone where we observed a portion of the ongoing trial of Charles Taylor, the former head of Liberia charged with among other crimes genocide and crimes against humanity; the work of the Organization or Security and Co-operation in Europe (OSCE); The Iran-U.S. Claims Tribunal; as well as the Asser Institute and the Hague Forum for Judicial Expertise.

We also toured the facilities and were briefed by a judge, prosecutor, and defense counsel of both the International Criminal Tribunal for the former Yugoslavia (ICTY) and the International Criminal Court (ICC). In addition, we observed a portion of the trial of the former deputy of the now-deceased Slobodan Milošević, who was representing himself by choice. All proceedings in those courts are translated in real-time into French and English.

Without exception, the people who briefed us were knowledgeable and of many races and nationalities. They were enthusiastic about their work, hopeful that their jobs are meaningful and their missions will be achieved, and thereby produce a better, more peaceful, and tolerant world through the application of the rule of law and communications between nations and their representatives.

Their presentations uniformly reflected what appeared to be a common mindset among them that to be realistic does not require that they abandon their ideals. Conversely, none of them appeared to be defensive about their work, their city, and the future of their organizations and tribunals despite some of the world's skepticism about their value, particularly that of the United States. Leadership in these organizations appeared to be awarded strictly on the basis of experience, intelligence, and industry and without reference to gender, race, or nationality.

The exposure to these international institutions and the competent and dedicated people who make them work as well as they do gave me new hope. It seemed like a world far apart from what I knew existed or understood and appreciated before I flew into Amsterdam that Sunday, September 21. We were greeted by mostly sunny days at The Hague, despite being told before we arrived that it rains there almost every day.

I must confess though that the one afternoon that we had off, literally and figuratively punctuated with an exclamation point the new spirit of hope for the future that I found on this trip. On that one afternoon, a group of judges traveled by train to Amsterdam. There, besides taking a boat tour of that beautiful city, we visited the Anne Frank House, which reminded us of the horrors that men are capable of inflicting on each other in the name of race, religion, and ethnicity.

This, of course, is what the institutions and people that we were learning about are working to prevent. It is also what can happen and still happens—genocide and crimes against humanity—when these institutions and people fail to institutionalize the application of the rule of law across the globe. This point was brought home in poignant visuals and words.

After witnessing the horrors visited upon Anne Frank and her family through her eyes and writing, we were confronted with a quote written by Primo Levi, a writer and Auschwitz survivor, as we were leaving the house:

> [O]ne single Anne Frank moves us more than the countless others who suffered just as she did, but whose faces have remained in the shadows. Perhaps it is better that way, if we were capable of taking in all the suffering of all those people, we would not be able to live.

Thank God, The Hague is working to enable us to live on and is shaping history and our hopes for the future.

Have a happy Thanksgiving.

Dispute Resolution and Access to Justice

The Intersection of Advocacy and Financial Forensics: The Role of the Expert in 21st Century Dispute Resolution
A Recovering Judge's Perspective

"Don't play in the other guy's analytical ballpark."

From the perspective of "a Recovering Judge," I appreciate this opportunity to discuss the role of the "expert" in the 21st century profession of dispute resolution. I spent a total of 29 years, from 1978 to 2007, on three different trial courts. I was also assigned to Maryland's intermediate appellate court on multiple occasions.

For the last 17 years, I have engaged in the world of private dispute resolution as an arbitrator, mediator, neutral case evaluator, special magistrate, and consultant on dispute resolution system design and implementation.

What I see is vastly different from what I saw from the Bench in the last quarter of the 20th century, 1978–1999, and the first decade of the 21st century, 2000–2007.

Like every other institution of government, the judiciary, as well as the private dispute resolution sector, is rapidly changing. "Evolving" connotes too slow a process to be an accurate description of what is going on. Technology and globalization are rapidly transforming the forums and techniques of dispute resolution and, with them, the paradigms of the administration of civil justice.

These modifications of existing governmental institutions, corporate organizations, as well as new financial products and devices, result from rapid technological development and globalization.

These trends, notwithstanding some of the subliminal messages from our recent election, will not be reversed. So, therefore, the role of "the expert" must necessarily expand and diversify to accommodate these changes and trends.

I recognize that it is ironic that almost contemporaneous with these changes, and my remarks, we just recently witnessed a not-significant portion of the electorate in this country (and if you want to count "Brexit," indeed the world) revolting at the voting booths against "elites." "Experts," I submit, are the very model of an "elite."

a. Changes in the Methods of Dispute Resolution

Traditionally, our citizens have had their disputes (legal and factual) resolved by a judge or jury in a courtroom. There, the role of the "expert" has historically focused on assisting the trier of fact, be it a judge or jury, to understand the evidence.

Those experts have not worked for the court and are not paid by the court. Rather, they work for and are paid by the parties, and, therefore, their opinions are, at least initially, viewed by both judges and juries as suspect. I am sure that almost everyone in this category has encountered that barrier, if not overt cynicism, to their opinions being received and found persuasive.

That is changing. For one thing, the appointment by the court of its own "experts," particularly in cases involving business valuation issues, is on the rise. Most state courts have the authority to do that and more and more are open to exercising it.

Courts also are increasingly utilizing financial forensic experts as Receivers and Special Magistrates. Most state courts and all federal courts give their judges the authority and discretion to appoint whomever they want, including non-lawyers, within the standard of "abuse of discretion." Appointing someone with knowledge of the issues and industry before the courts and who can make informed and educated recommendations or even run a company for the court, and having the experience to do so, is clearly not an "abuse of discretion."

Finally, the courts are increasingly utilizing Special Magistrates, or as we now call them Magistrates and Settlement Administrators a/k/a "Claims Adjudicators," to administer and manage settlements of high stakes, multiparty litigation, particularly class-action cases and mass tort cases.

Court-appointed Special Magistrates and Settlement Administrators are, most of the time, authorized by rule and/or court order to employ "such professionals, experts and consultants as they deem necessary" to carry out their court-ordered duties, which likely will include recommending the allocation of damages, expert fees, and attorney's fees to the court.

The best-known example of this relatively recent phenomenon is Ken Feinberg, an attorney who has overseen numerous compensation programs to pay the victims and their families after tragedies and corporate mishaps, such as 9/11, the 2013 Boston Marathon bombing, the BP Gulf Oil Spill, to name a few. In each of these cases, and others, the role of Financial Forensic Experts has been to perform the following, among other functions:

- Develop formulas and algorithms to determine the allocation of economic damages based on severity indexes established by the terms of the settlement agreement and data collected to support it.

- Explain to the Special Magistrate, the Administrator, and/or the court, those formulas and the allocation of damage awards based thereon.

- Explain to the recipients of the different categories and amounts of damage the basis for the differentiations in the size of their distribution or award.

- Supervise the transfer and application of data from investigations, interviews, and records to the administrators formulating and implementing the settlement.

I have been involved in this process more than once as a Special Magistrate and Settlement Administrator, and I can tell you that the market is growing for these Financial Forensic Experts who are qualified to and willing to perform these functions; but the number of potential experts who are qualified to do so by education and experience is not large or at least not known.

b. The Use of Experts in ADR

Furthermore, the non-traditional use of experts is growing, particularly the use of Financial Forensic Experts, in what is known as alternative dispute resolution (ADR). These new roles derive from the traditional role of assisting a judge or jury but are expanded to include persuading other players in the dispute.

For example, in mediation, the expert can be most effective by assisting the opposing party, opposing counsel, or even the opposing expert in understanding the issues from the client's perspective or how a court would understand it. There's an old saying in the litigation world:

Don't play in the other guy's analytical ballpark.

However, in mediation, you *do* play in the other guy's analytical ballpark. That's how you persuade him or her. If successful, it is likely that you will have a winner.

In an arbitration, examples would be explaining to a single arbitrator or a three-arbitrator panel the methodology that is appropriate to value market share in order to determine the percent of allocation of damages between defendants—as in asbestos cases or in the newly emerging cannabis industry—or the percentage of revenue or profits to which a consultant is entitled.

The success of the expert's client will very much depend on the expert's ability to persuade the arbitrator that the methodology utilized is appropriate and individualized to the valuation of the real, personal, or even intellectual property at issue in the case and not just a one-size-fits-all formula developed by the industry, particularly the insurance industry.

Finally, it is useful to understand that in the new paradigm, the expert opinions that will be sought will, to a certain extent, depend on the dispute resolution forum and technique being utilized by the parties and counsel.

In litigation and arbitration, an expert's opinion will be sought as to the specific quantification of damages utilizing the theory of the case and the valuation theory selected by the hiring authority. In a mediation or neutral case evaluation, an expert opinion is most likely to be sought to aid in a risk analysis designed to leverage the possible settlement of the case.

I hope I have been helpful and have adequately described the comparatively new world that the premiere Financial Forensic Experts have been or will shortly be operating in. As we look to the future of the field of dispute resolution and the administration of justice, perhaps the best guidance that I can provide is the advice of Abraham Lincoln, which we would all do well to heed today:

> *The dogmas of the quiet past are inadequate for the stormy present and future. As our circumstances are new, we must think anew and get anew.*

Chapter 13

Confronting Complexity: The Role of Judges and Mediators in an Increasingly Complicated World
'Separate But Equal, Different Yet Complementary'

*"Neutrality is central to the value we add as
ADR Professionals and it is what allows us
to earn the trust of all sides in a dispute."*

This writer's 21st century "branding" is "Senior Judge" when I am recalled to sit as a trial court judge or as a mediator for the Court of Special Appeals or one of the trial courts in Maryland. When I am not recalled, I function and am referred to as a "mediator" or "arbitrator" in the private sector. As such, I mediate or arbitrate disputes that may or may not be filed as cases in state or federal court. By definition and by court rule, I am not "practicing law," which allows me to function in these multiple capacities in our criminal and civil justice system, although not historically without some degree of controversy.

With this background and experience, I noticed two books that evoke very distinctive yet complementary themes. One book, *Politics, Dialogue and the Evolution of Democracy*, is authored by the renowned Ken Cloke, whom I have had the pleasure of meeting and learning from on the subject of "coaching" conflict resolution. This book reflects on the role and necessary level of objectivity or neutrality required of an alternative dispute resolution (ADR) professional seeking to mediate the escalating and intense political conflict in the United States.

The other book is entitled *TOUGH CASES–Judges Tell the Stories of Some of the Hardest Decisions They've Ever Made.* This book, edited by Russell F. Canan, Gregory E. Mize, and Frederick H. Weisberg, themselves state and D.C. trial court judges, and written by 13 trial court judges, candidly discusses the complexity and the inherent difficulty caused by the uncertainty surrounding what the resolution of these "tough" cases should be.

Both of these books are even more topical and important if considered in the context of remarks by the late Judge Learned Hand, whom many, including this writer, believe to have been the nation's foremost jurist never nominated to the U.S. Supreme Court. Judge Hand said in 1944 as the nation waged World War II:

> *The spirit of liberty is the spirit which is not too sure it is right.*

Well, what happened to the "spirit of liberty" in the 21st century?

It is either extinct or well hidden; hopefully, the latter! At best, it is lost or indecipherable in a sea of "Talking Points," which ignore or evade complex political, economic, sociological, technological, and psychological issues by rhetorically simplifying or trivializing those issues so that their complexity goes unnoticed.

Isn't that what we are witnessing in the latest exhibition of this phenomenon—the political theater and accompanying drama over the "Government Shutdown" and "The Wall," which are being played out before a captive, unwilling, and unwelcoming cast of 800,000 federal workers, whose price of admission includes, at least temporarily, their livelihoods and ability to plan for their families' futures?

Statements, such as "we need the wall to have Border Security," "open the Government first–then we'll negotiate," and "the Wall is immoral," do not even acknowledge, let alone address, the dimensions of the multidisciplinary complexity of the issues that must be understood and discussed in order to resolve this situation/crisis.

What they do in absolute terms without even a modicum of humility is say, "I'm sure I'm right and you are wrong," which is antithetical to the "spirit of liberty" Judge Learned Hand described so eloquently in the middle of a real crisis: World War II.

This attitude is noted even in the judiciary. Professor Dan Kahan of Yale Law School points out that while judges may acknowledge complexity and even uncertainty with their law clerks and, in some instances, colleagues in chambers, their decisions and their opinions explaining them more often than not "strike a pose of exact certitude."

The state court trial judges writing in their book, *TOUGH CASES*, however, refreshingly confirm, as the editors point out in their introduction, that their book aims "to demystify judicial decision-making and to make the process accessible and understandable to ordinary people who would not otherwise get a ringside seat. They succeed!

These authors only lament is their observation that because the judiciary is so "intensely hierarchical," this humility is not widely shared at the highest levels of the judiciary, particularly at the federal level.

Their book illuminates the fact that lower court judges have much to teach judicial officers at the most elite levels of the judiciary about the importance of acknowledging complexity and difficulty. This is a hue and cry that I have no doubt my fellow "lower court judges" will enthusiastically, but with the requisite humility, echo loudly and clearly whenever a forum is available to do so.

That said, the demystifying of the federal judicial decision-making process, if implemented, might also dramatically reduce the vitriol and distrust expanding exponentially with the lack of humility observable in the confirmation process for federal appellate and U.S. Supreme Court judges and justices.

The inherent and increasing complexity of political issues in the United States, whether they are to be decided by the legislative or executive branches of government or some arguably hybrid combination of the two, raises serious issues for those of us whose profession is conflict resolution and who could provide conflict resolution services to those involved in political and/or governmental disputes.

As Ken Cloke cites in his book, *Politics*, the fundamental question of who is qualified to mediate political issues and public disputes depends on the disputant's perception of what constitutes "neutrality."

One view is best articulated by Professor Lawrence Susskind, founder of the Consensus Building Institute at MIT and a professor in the Program on Negotiation at Harvard Law School:

> *Neutrality is central to the value we add as ADR Professionals and it is what allows us to earn the trust of all sides in a dispute.*

In a nutshell, Professor Susskind's view is that if you have taken a position and it is known, "there is no way anyone who disagrees with your position(s) will accept you as Mediator that they can trust."

That view is contrasted with the opinion of Professor Bernie Mayer of Creighton University, who has written extensively on conflict resolution. Professor Mayer's position is that it is not necessary for a "Neutral" to totally surrender or repress all of his or her political, moral, and ethical beliefs in order to mediate or facilitate dialogues involving persons with opposing ideas and views, as long as the "Neutral" exudes sufficient humility to project his or her sincere belief that he or she "is not too sure he or she is 100% right"—*i.e.*, the "spirit of liberty" as Judge Learned Hand described it.

That means that the "Neutral" must find constructive, diplomatic, practical, and effective methods to confront unacceptable behavior and languages—such as bullying, blackmail, and intimidation—while still being willing to recognize that people who behave and speak in these unacceptable ways can and do still have legitimate concerns that should be addressed.

In other words, it is not and should not be required that as a mediator, I should completely surrender my personal views in order to effectively mediate or facilitate a dialogue between persons with opposing views to my own.

Bottom line, in the words of anthropologist Laura Nader, it is not necessary to "trade justice for harmony." That said, before any ADR professional undertakes to mediate or arbitrate a dispute of any kind, but particularly one with a political component, the ADR professional's neutrality if questioned should be discussed fully and thereafter unconditionally accepted by all parties and counsel or the case should not be accepted by the mediator.

I have engaged in those types of discussions with both parties and counsel, when requested, as a part of the "Neutral" selection process in various types of cases, including commercial and professional liability claims and disputes, some with a political component.

Without exception, those discussions have been substantive, without rancor, and in good faith. They have also resulted in a better-quality "Neutral" selection process than would have occurred if they had not taken place; and at the end of the day, they have increased the likelihood of the underlying dispute being resolved.

Chapter 14

Access to Justice and the Management of Expectations

"[I]nflated expectations are a by-product of our focus on providing greater 'access to justice' to individuals and institutions, who do not completely understand and accept the constitutional, statutory, and practical limitations of our judicial branch of government."

For the last 25 years, there is one theme that has been echoed more than any other at judicial conferences and bar association meetings, federal, state and local, as well as strategic planning sessions conducted by every organized judicial and legal organization from Maryland Legal Aid, to law schools, to the decisions of the Judicial Disabilities Commission. That theme is that lawyers and judges should always be working to increase access to justice. Indeed, it would likely constitute heresy to the profession to suggest otherwise.

However, I hope this is not viewed as an attack on that goal when I say that I hope that recognizing that the rhetoric and the actions taken to "increase access to justice" have created heightened and, at times, unrealistic expectations among our citizens about the ability of courts and other public dispute resolution institutions to solve everyone's problems.

The goal is, on balance, a good one—worthy of our collective and individual attention and energy. That said, increasing access to justice will proceed more smoothly if we contemporaneously address and temper the enhanced expectations created by that effort honestly and forthrightly.

The results of this focus are very visible. The creation of the family divisions in Maryland's circuit courts in the mid-1990s after years of advocacy was the first accomplishment. Then followed other specialized courts including, but not limited to, Drug Courts, Mental Health Courts, Veterans Courts, and other adjunct and specialty Case Management Programs, all coordinated by an Office of Problem-Solving Courts housed in the Administrative Offices of the Courts.

The emergence and development of these "Problem-Solving Courts" have proceeded on a parallel time track with our judiciary, enabling, indeed encouraging, our citizens to represent themselves (self-represent) in court proceedings. These proceedings, at times, include arguably complex cases that might even challenge a lawyer's knowledge and ability to manage.

The judiciary has done this despite what former Court of Special Appeals Judge Theodore Bloom repeatedly referred to in his opinions presciently as "the perils of pro-se practice." The judiciary has done so by providing forms, which can be used to commence, respond to, and maintain litigation; and the judiciary has presented "How To" programs that attempt to instruct litigants, who are not legally trained, on how to handle their self-represented cases in court.

Also emerging, over the last 25–30 years, and developing during roughly the same timeframe, was the comparatively new field and profession of alternative dispute resolution or ADR. All of these trends and developments have proceeded from the premise that a satisfactory resolution of peoples' disputes, more often than not, should deal not just with the dispute itself, but with the underlying causes of the dispute.

The underlying cause of most disputes is usually more economic and psychological than it is legal or even factual, except when the psychology and/or the economics drive the law and the facts.

The enhanced expectation that not only will our citizens' disputes be resolved, but the underlying causes of those disputes will be addressed, is one that is evolving among all classes of disputants and litigants in our courts as well as in the halls of our administrative agencies, ADR conference rooms, and even in our legislatures.

Without question, these inflated expectations are a by-product of our focus on providing greater "access to justice" to individuals and institutions, which do not completely understand and accept the constitutional, statutory, and practical limitations of our judicial branch of government. It also results from the hue and cry from all segments of society to reduce the time and costs of dispute resolution generally, and litigation particularly, both in the short and long term.

The result of those enhanced expectations that disputes should not just be resolved, but that they should be resolved in a manner that economically and efficiently addresses their cause so that they will not recur, is that the public and private institutions—including law firms and courts that have been developed in our society to assist people in resolving their disputes—are being forced to dramatically change their business models and work processes to accommodate those enhanced expectations.

That process is ongoing and far from perfected or even complete; nor is progress uniform even from country to country, state to state, or even county to county in our own state of Maryland.

Individuals and institutions, including judges, clerks, administrators, and regulators, in our justice system have not uniformly adapted to their changing roles particularly where litigants are self-represented; and those roles are, at best, not clear in certain situations. That has recently been exhibited in Judicial Disabilities Commission cases, among others.

Finally, new methods of dispute resolution are emerging and increasingly being utilized by parties, including many who could still afford to pay for full-blown litigation or arbitration but choose not to.

The judiciary will soon have to determine whether it will offer these arguably more efficient and economical dispute resolution techniques through qualified and trained practitioners or leave them strictly to the private ADR sector, which is already embracing them.

Chapter 15

Lessons from the Conflict Resolution Profession to the World of Politics

"It shouldn't be about you, so get over yourself."

By the time this column is published, Donald J. Trump will have been inaugurated as the 45th president of the United States. As he takes office, professional polls across the country, indeed the world, reflect a lot more agreement among the populace with the outlines of his proposed policies than his detractors would like to believe, and a lot more anxiety about his temperament, *e.g.,* his readily apparent and blatant narcissism and its potential effect on his decision-making processes and his priorities, than his admirers would like to think or care about.

With no sign of the soon-to-be presidential "Tweet Wars" being abated by Donald J. Trump in consideration of the assumption of the burdens of the presidency—not to mention his new online battles with civil rights icon Congressman John Lewis, former California Governor Arnold Schwarzenegger, and actress Meryl Streep having been initiated—time management could become a critical issue for the new president, especially between the tweeting time of midnight and 4:00 am and during the time normally reserved for Intelligence Briefings.

All this distracts from the most important point, which is that the toxic political atmosphere in our country is, without question, interfering without capacity to solve pressing problems.

As former Arizona Court of Appeals Judge Bruce E. Meyerson, now writer, mediator, arbitrator, and trainer, points out:

> *Problem-solving, which we do every day as Neutrals, is never made easier when those in dispute attack the motives, integrity, or character of others.*

These verbal attacks are described as "Unproductive Communication" by Christopher Moore in his classic text, *The Mediation Process.*

Inject this "unproductive communication" into the larger world of politics and we see the cause-and-effect relationship of over-the-top political rhetoric; commercials with references to "Second Amendment Remedies; and websites that put the crosshairs of a rifle on "targeted" congressional districts to the points of impasse on so many challenges facing our country and state.

These messages preaching intolerance emanate from both the left and the right fringes of our politics. They bring credit to neither. As Jim Leach, former Iowa Republican congressman and chair of the National Endowment of the Humanities, has written presciently: "Words matter!"

Stirring anger and playing on the irrational fears of citizens inflames hate; when coupled with character assassination, polarizing rhetoric can exacerbate intolerance without, in any way, facilitating problem-solving and respect for other points of view.

The conflict resolution profession has some very valuable insight and lessons to offer in this environment. As retired Judge Meyerson said at a recent panel discussion at Emory University on "Civility in American Politics":

> *Skillful communication can turn information into power and conflict into opportunities for greater understanding, more meaningful solutions, and a stronger sense of community.*

Indeed, it can! And for that reason, perhaps we ought to distribute Judge Myerson's remarks to the members of Congress and our state legislature with a training video on how to "skillfully communicate."

There is, however, an interesting dissent to this viewpoint that is illustrated by a colleague and friend, F. Peter Phillips, a mediator and blogger in New Jersey. In his blog, Phillips notes that at its core, the question is, "Can a public leader be a problem-solver while still leading?"

The answer is debatable.

The debate highlights the differences in the role of a mediator and political leader. For example, a political leader advocates policy and seeks public support for it; a mediator (in theory) has no view as to what the outcome of a dispute ought to be.

Having been entrusted with power by being elected or appointed, a political leader advances policy in the face of opposition from other political factions; a mediator (in theory) treats disputing parties even-handedly and without regard to his or her own interests or point of view.

Finally, a political leader in our representative democracy is empowered to advance certain articulated goals; a mediator (in theory) seeks only to help the disputants identify a mutually beneficial outcome to a conflict so they can return to more socially productive endeavors.

The question is, then, do these distinctions compel the conclusion that political leadership necessitates belligerence?

Former President Barack Obama campaigned for the presidency promising to rise above partisanship, *i.e.*, all conflict, and become the person who would reconcile divided parties: the Israelis and the Palestinians, the Pakistanis and the Indians, and closer to home, our very own Republicans and Democrats.

During his first two years, at best, he had some directional progress, but little demonstrable success abroad. At home, he pointedly abandoned any pretense to being a mediator probably as a result of a combination of necessity and frustration to push legislation on healthcare, financial regulation, and stimulus.

His inability to reconcile his two roles as political leader and mediator/reconciler (Unifier) explain his inability to play both roles and may well have caused him, and more directly his political party, to lose significant electoral support among independents who wanted him to be a mediator.

His party, on the other hand, may have lost a portion of its base on the left who wanted him and his nominated successor, Hillary Clinton, to be strictly a political leader.

The president and his political party's failure to reconcile these two roles left the county at the mercy of the promises of the populist "negotiator," who campaigned as neither a mediator nor a political leader, but rather a "fixer" whose policies largely remain unknown and unpredictable ("only I can fix it"), as well as unhinged or even coherently related to any economic or political philosophy.

As F. Peter Phillips points out, the test of the success of a mediator is whether he or she achieves a "mutual level of dissatisfaction among the settling disputants." The very different test of a leader is whether he or she effects change.

These two measures inevitably yield two helpful (if perhaps unwelcome) truths. The first is that the power of a leader achieves its highest social utility when it is exercised. The other is that you can't effectively and credibly mediate a case, an issue, or a policy if you want it to come out in a certain way.

This, in turn, yields a universal lesson to both political leaders and mediators for very different reasons. It shouldn't be about you, so get over yourself. Whether and when that lesson will be learned by the new president and his administration, and how, remains to be seen!

Growth of Cannabis Plants Fertilizes Legal and ADR Business

"I'd ask you what you are smoking,
but we already know."

If you think lawyers who are creative, indeed entrepreneurial, should be encouraged to ply their trade, and that emerging industries are fertile ground to do so, then you should give a shout-out to the rapidly expanding business of manufacturing, packaging, selling, and distribution of cannabis for medicinal and recreational purposes.

More states, including Maryland, are legalizing cannabis for multiple purposes. These jurisdictions are providing forums for the creation and development of new and, in some cases, eclectic business relationships. These include consulting agreements, distribution deals, partnerships, licensing relationships, and even the co-authoring of "How-to Manuals."

Like all other business dealings and organizations created for the purpose of developing new and different products for profit, the potential for disputes to arise between partners, competitors, and parties working together one day and competing against each other the next is present.

Due to the nature of the cannabis industry and its multiple levels and conflicting state and federal regulatory schemes, many individuals and businesses are choosing to use alternative dispute resolution (ADR) instead of litigating when troubles or disputes arise. This is for a variety of reasons.

For one, there is a perception, or at least a concern, among the individuals and business organizations that are invested in this emerging industry (as well as many of the lawyers and law firms who may represent them) that judges and juries who don't "like" them or "don't like" what they do for historical and/or cultural reasons may "punish" them, *i.e.*, not give them a fair hearing in their case.

This perception can be effectively addressed by private mediation and/or arbitration by one or more "Neutrals" agreed upon by the parties and who hopefully have some knowledge of the industry.

This perception leads cannabis industry entrepreneurs to insert into their contracts, mandatory mediation and arbitration clauses designed to avoid these negative possibilities.

Mediation, by its inherent nature, as well as, in certain situations, by statute, rule, or contract, includes a confidentiality component. Confidentiality, as the state of Delaware found out the hard way, is prohibited in public dispute resolution forums, *i.e.*, the courts. Private arbitration, on the other hand, can be confidential if agreed upon and mandated accordingly by contract or by ADR provider rules.

Confidentiality is very important if the activity, or even part of the activity that is the subject of the dispute, remains illegal under federal law even if it is legal in many states. This is the case with most of the activities associated with the cannabis industry. Evidence of this includes the refusal of most banks and other traditional financial institutions to finance the development of the industry and the companies that are forming within it.

This reality is further evidenced by the refusal of colleges and universities to offer training to those who work in the medical marijuana industry. It is noteworthy that the most recent example of this trend was our own University of Maryland School of Pharmacy, acting on the advice of the Maryland Attorney General's Office, cancelling plans to offer training for those who work in the medical marijuana industry.

This development has necessitated medical marijuana industry entrepreneurs and workers to search elsewhere for education and training on everything from how to set up their businesses, to how to grow, store, transport, market, and sell their product, as well as bookkeeping of their businesses, while staying within the law, *i.e.*, not running afoul of conflicting federal and state regulations of their businesses.

They have found, by process of elimination, that the only sources for that education and training are other individuals and companies located in states that legalized medical and, in some cases, recreational marijuana use in previous years. These individuals and companies have the education, background, and most importantly the experience to provide the education and training needed to establish and develop potentially profitable medical marijuana enterprises here.

The result has been that these new entrepreneurs and their businesses are negotiating and entering into consulting contracts with experienced individuals and companies in the medical marijuana industry in other states in order to obtain information and training. These contracts are not easily crafted and understood even by lawyers familiar with the industry.

The relationships created by the contracts between the consulting companies and those who avail themselves of their services to provide start-up training are often fraught with the risk of the disclosure of trade secrets, as well as the violation of covenants not to compete, etc. In turn, the contracts often have provisions drafted to minimize, if not eliminate, those risks.

They are not always successful, which, in turn, creates conflicts that if not resolved quickly and efficiently can kill an emerging medical marijuana business before it gets started. The result has been mediation and arbitrations generated by the dispute resolution provisions in these consulting contracts.

I have been involved as both a mediator and an arbitrator in a number of these cases involving lawyers and parties from across the country. Intermingled with these is litigation filed in multiple federal courts in an attempt to either consolidate, in a geographically convenient or perceived friendly forum, the cases involving identical parties or third parties spun off for tactical reasons from other parties.

Indeed, my favorite case and experience so far is the one in which the parties and counsel sought dismissal or transfer of a case in which I was the chair of a three-arbitrator panel. They first sought that relief from the U.S. District Court in Washington, D.C., which not only declined to dismiss or transfer our arbitration case, but instead ordered the parties to proceed before my panel in Maryland or D.C.

The losing party then came to our panel requesting the same relief. When we realized they were asking the panel to, in effect, reverse the U.S. District Court's decision, my only comment on behalf of the panel was, "I'd ask you what you are smoking, but we already know." This statement, of course, accompanied our negative decision.

Chapter 17

Arbitration That Works: Careful Selection Is the Key

*"Last time I checked, three arbitrators cost
more than one."*

There are many organizations that are in the market willing to administer your future arbitration for a fee, which usually includes an "administration fee" in addition to the actual arbitrator's fee. They include AAA, JAMS, ICC, CPR, FINRA, and IAA, among others.

In addition, there are numerous individual arbitrators and smaller "groups" that these larger providers refer to as the "ad hoc" market. Some of these charge administrative fees and some do not. All provide arbitrators and/or mediators at their own individual rates.

Many of the established institutional providers have developed their own rules, procedures, and protocols for handling different types of disputes as well as rates adjusted for the size, type, and complexity of the dispute.

The "ad hoc" providers, consisting of individuals and small groups loosely associated with each other for the purpose of consolidating their administrative costs, usually don't have their own rules, but have the ability to administer an arbitration under any rules agreed upon by the parties and their counsel and can also assist in customizing specific rules and protocols, including scheduling, discovery, motions practice, and even payment tailored to the particular dispute.

Yet, as I have pointed out, in many cases, little if any thought or time is allocated for investigation by counsel of the comparative ability and resources as well as fees of an organization, individual arbitrator, or ad hoc provider to resolve a particular dispute efficiently and economically.

As attorney Erika C. Birg, a partner in Nelson, Mullins Riley & Scarborough's Atlanta office, has often noted, the "arbitration provision" of a business agreement is "drafted at the last minute, when all that coffee has worn off and the eyelids are starting to droop. The determination of who will referee, let alone judge the dispute, is often not considered at all, and the first organization that comes to mind is selected."

That is quite often a mistake that will haunt the lawyer and the client who dozed off too quickly; there are important issues to consider:

- Is there a good fit between the organization and/or arbitrator(s) selected and the size, complexity, and subject matter of the dispute? Included in this deliberation should be whether you want one or three arbitrators. Last time I checked, three arbitrators cost more than one.

- How are the arbitrators to be selected by the parties; by the organization, etc.?

- Does the individual and/or organizational provider have subject matter expertise?

- What are the payment arrangements available?

- Further, can the provider service your parties, witnesses, and counsel in the geographic area most convenient to them and are the arbitrator and the provider adequately staffed to provide teleconferencing and/or video-testimony as well as travel if necessary?

- Finally, and perhaps most importantly, particularly if you are considering one of the larger and established organizations that has its own set of rules, can you and do you want to be bound to those rules?

For example, international rules typically require all witness statements and evidence to be submitted in advance of the hearing. As a result, there is usually little direct testimony to be given. This contrasts with the commercial rules of the American Arbitration Association (AAA), which allow a basic type of "notice pleading" and a streamlined procedure, including a hearing.

The AAA has different rules for construction and employment cases as well as rules allowing "dispositive motions" under certain conditions and optional provisions to agree in advance to an "appeal" to a panel of retired judges to review an arbitration award.

This can make a significant difference to counsel or a client who wants a streamlined dispute resolution, but at the same time to preserve an economically viable method to challenge an unfair award.

The bottom line is that arbitration is intended to be a cost-effective and efficient process. Notwithstanding the criticism of the process in recent years, the evidence is that if it is managed properly, it still can be and is.

The parties and counsel, however, have to exercise their responsibility to carefully select the provider and the arbitrator who can most efficiently and economically get the job done.

Chapter 18

Which ADR Technique? Choose Carefully

"So, Buyer Beware! You make an uncomfortable arbitral bed, you lie in it!"

Which dispute resolution technique should parties and their counsel use in the courthouse or conference room of the future? The short answer is the classic lawyer's response: It depends!

The decision to use alternative dispute resolution (ADR) and even the choice of which ADR technique to employ is often made by a business client who, thinking he or she is saving money, unknowingly at his or her peril includes a "form" dispute resolution clause in the commercial documents in an attempt to anticipate problems that might arise in the transaction and/or business relationship.

That "form" dispute resolution clause is often pulled from a book, which should be titled *Dispute Resolution Clauses for Dummies*, and prepared without the assistance of counsel. This usually means it is included in the contract without a full understanding of its ramifications.

A poorly conceived and drafted dispute resolution clause in a contract can wreak havoc on the operations and finances of even the better-run business organizations. This is true even when counsel is involved. I have observed countless cases as a judge, and now as a private mediator and arbitrator, where the dispute resolution clause was drafted by a primarily transactional lawyer without consulting the litigator who ultimately would have to work within the confines of the language in the clause if a dispute arose. This inevitably puts the client in an unnecessarily exposed position.

Business cases, labor disputes, buy-sell agreements, franchise agreements, and particularly employment disputes, arise in many contexts that have not been anticipated, and for that reason are not governed by the dispute resolution clause inserted in a contract without much thought.

These claims and the defenses to them each carry a unique potential for their own narrative, which can develop into drama in the hands of capable litigators, parties, and witnesses in a forum that favors such a presentation. Therefore, it would behoove the prudent business or individual client and his or her careful and thoughtful transactional lawyer, after consultation with the experienced litigator down the hall, to think about the choice of dispute resolution mechanisms and providers before typing and pressing the print key on the desktop to insert the final version in their contract.

That means it is wise to keep in mind how the client and any witnesses are likely to present before different types of audiences. Will they naturally make a good impression on a judge or jury? If not, then an arbitration perhaps preceded by a mediation probably is a better choice because it would be easier to guide clients and witnesses in these more intimate and less formal ADR settings than in a courtroom.

The consequences of not being careful or not being able to visualize how a particular dispute resolution protocol and provider would play out in the future have recently become much more apparent because of the "Deflate-gate" case played out on the national stage. As a result of allegations that New England Patriot quarterback Tom Brady ordered/aided/abetted the deflating of one or more footballs in the Patriots playoff game with the Seattle Seahawks, the arbitration provision negotiated by the NFL Players Association with the NFL became operational. This resulted in a proceeding before Arbitration Commissioner Roger Goodell, who arguably was arbitrary and capricious in the conduct of the arbitration hearing and the imposition of a four-game suspension on Brady. That was the view of U.S. District Court Judge Richard M. Berman who nullified the suspension on the grounds that the conduct of the arbitration, albeit arguably allowed under the arbitration provision of the collective bargaining agreement, was unfair and therefore null and void.

That ruling was reversed by a three-judge panel of the U.S. Court of Appeals for the Second Circuit, which held, "The Commissioner properly exercised his broad discretion under the collective bargaining agreement and that his procedural rulings were properly grounded in that agreement and did not deprive Brady of fundamental fairness."

This latest ruling by a divided panel of the Second Circuit (2–1) basically sent the message that if you aren't careful and agree to a private arbitral procedure and/or provider that results in an unfair proceeding and result, you're bound by what you agreed to. So, Buyer Beware! You make an uncomfortable arbitral bed, you lie in it!

Chapter 19

Litigation vs. ADR: Different Strokes for Different Folks

*"Which dispute resolution technique should
the parties use in the multi-door courthouse
or conference room of the future?"*

I have described the cultural, economic, and structural changes in the legal and business communities that have transposed alternative dispute resolution (ADR) from a "cross-practice," which litigators engage in when they are contractually required or court-ordered to do so, to a fully integrated but increasingly separate and distinct set of dispute resolution services to be offered by law firms or other private "dispute resolution firms," "groups," and "individual professionals."

The judiciary also has, albeit belatedly, in the last 25 years recognized this primarily economic, but also legal and political reality, and begun to provide or at least encourage individual and corporate litigants to seek cost-effective and time-sensitive alternatives to full-blown litigation.

That trend is now firmly in place and developing to the point where even some courts, specifically the Chancery Court in Delaware, have begun to formally offer other dispute resolution services as alternatives to their traditional inventory of services. Until recently, courts restricted the services they offered to litigation and "settlement conferencing." The Delaware Chancery Court has expanded this to institutionalize arbitration, evaluative mediation, and neutral case evaluation services by the "Sitting Chancellors."

This has produced a further change to the structure, operations, and culture of mid-size to large law firms, albeit slowly, because of entrenched resistance based on law office economics and egos. For example, under the prevailing law firm business models and processes, transactions belonged to the "Corporate Department," wills and trusts to "Trusts & Estates (T&E)," and Bankruptcy to its own discrete practice areas or boutique law firms. Within these typical structures, "disputes" have been the exclusive domain of the litigators.

It should not be surprising to encounter resistance to this change by litigators who have historically settled most of their cases (98 percent) without help from a third-party neutral, either privately retained or court-imposed. Many litigators, on their own, have adapted to the changing client expectations for a faster and less expensive resolution of their disputes by engaging in more extensive and intense settlement negotiations as a part of the litigation process, or what Robert Margulies, a business litigator in New Jersey, refers to as "Litigotiation."[1]

This resistance and the reason for it, however, are based on a fundamental misunderstanding of the purpose and processes of ADR. What those who resist the expansion of the techniques utilized to resolve disputes beyond the traditional litigation process, even when it includes a large element of "litigotiation," do not comprehend is that the use of these ADR techniques is not just to settle the specific dispute before them but to resolve latent client goals and concerns that have led to their dispute.

---

[1] A term originally attributed to Marc Galanter, "Worlds of Deals: Using Negotiation to Teach About Legal Process," 34 J. LEGAL EDUC. 268, 268 (1984).

These other concerns almost always include addressing the underlying causes of the dispute as a means of preventing future conflict between the parties or even with third parties.

This is not always the case, as, for example, where the dispute is purely over money, such as in negligence cases resulting from automobile accidents, etc.

But even in cases where professional liability issues are to be resolved, there are clearly other issues and interests to be addressed—besides purely dollars and the merits and value of the claims and defenses. These can include reaching a resolution that does not engender future litigation or conflict between the policyholder and the carrier, as well as future underwriting issues between the policyholder and the carrier. There also can be issues and interests involved related to professional discipline and registration.

The resolution of these issues is not easily achieved by the standard "position-based" settlement negotiations that typically occur at various stages of a case being litigated. Furthermore, it is clear to anyone who has engaged in both—settlement discussions between litigators with multiple and alternating agendas are of a different nature and quality than those led by a qualified neutral ADR professional committed to only finding an amicable comprehensive resolution to the dispute and the underlying cause of it.

The former is most often intermittent, limited, not concentrated (mixed in with litigation issues), and unfocused on a comprehensive resolution. The latter is structured, concentrated, and focused solely on a comprehensive settlement of all issues, including those that caused the dispute to occur in the first place.

Litigators who are not trained as mediators are also likely to confine their position-based negotiations to remedies available through the court in which the litigation is filed. This arbitrarily restricts the ability of the parties to satisfactorily and comprehensively resolve their dispute in a way that addresses the underlying issues that produced the conflict and, in turn, eliminate the conditions that might create future controversies.

Finally, particularly in Maryland, position-based negotiations directly between lawyers acting as advocates for their clients are, of necessity, constrained by case law from the Maryland Court of Appeals. This case law in effect makes the issue a "jury question" as to whether an attorney for a party who recommended a settlement based on what an "expert" now says was "insufficient information" can be held liable.

This exposes lawyers to professional liability if there is not universal acceptance that he or she complied with the standard of care within the "Expert Witness Community" whose ads can be found in many legal magazines.

This exposure, as a practical matter, can be limited if not eliminated by skillful drafting of retainer agreements and/or settlement agreements. But if it is not, then the attorney, in order to insulate him- or herself from a future adverse finding by a jury (not made up of other lawyers), will instinctively refuse or at least delay engaging in settlement discussions that may also be limited for these same reasons.

This will have the effect of adding both unnecessary time and expense to the conduct of the case before even discussing settlement.

Which dispute resolution technique should the parties use in the multi-door courthouse or conference room of the future?

Chapter 20

The New and Improved Resolution of Disputes

*"[M]ediation in certain complex business disputes
can take days, weeks, or even months
and sometimes has to be staged."*

Corporate in-house counsel, law firms, and individuals are looking for cost-effective alternatives to full blown litigation. Law firms will have to provide them in order to survive. Courts will have to incorporate them into the dispute resolution services they offer in order to remain relevant, lest they be replaced by private alternatives or worse become the lower tier of an economically tiered civil justice system.

The Chancery Court of Delaware has been out in front of the curve. That court, which essentially is a Business Court and at least in part a model for other Business Courts around the country including the Maryland Business & Technology Case Management Program, has in the last year begun to allow parties to choose arbitration as an alternative to litigation in front of its chancellors.

Although it had a temporary set-back when its arbitration option was ruled "unconstitutional" essentially because its proceedings were not public, that issue has now been addressed. The Chancery Court offers an evaluative form of mediation of its cases by a chancellor who will not preside over the case. More Business Courts around the country, including our own, will and surely should follow suit.

There are many different models of Business Courts, Commercial Parts, Business Technology Case Management Programs, Complex Litigation Management Tracks, etc., in this country. Each has its own history and culture based on that history. All were created because the "business litigation" and the "business disputes" that give rise to the cases filed in these courts, as well as the parties and lawyers participating in them, were perceived to have "special needs." Those "special needs" were articulated in the halls of state legislatures and the rules committee rooms in many of our state's highest courts where these specialized dockets were conceived, born, and developed to various stages of maturity across the country.

The "special needs" of the parties and counsel in business cases in all of these states are identified as more timely, rational, legally correct, and predictable. It is also important that these disputes be resolved or decided in a manner that recognizes that unlike many other types of cases, an untimely, or arbitrarily and unduly delayed, resolution of a case or dispute may devastate one or both of the parties' ability to continue to operate, particularly in an economy such as the one we're in now.

Similarly, a legally incorrect, impractical, or illogical ruling particularly on a request for temporary restraining order (TRO) or a preliminary injunction can unfairly and irreparably leverage a business party's position so that it cannot recover legally and, more importantly, financially and operationally.

Legally incorrect, illogical, and/or untimely, *e.g.*, unduly delayed resolutions of business disputes, unnecessarily cause great difficulty for business organizations when it comes to accurately quantifying risk going forward in their operations—not just in specific cases but generally.

Alternative dispute resolution (ADR) has been integrated into all of these "Business Courts" as a means of meeting these needs in various forms:

- Formal "*Settlement Conferences*" are not "mediations," for, among other reasons, insufficient time is allotted by the courts to conduct mediation. In fact, in many instances, not enough time is allotted to have a meaningful settlement conference. Unfortunately, the number of cases processed is deemed to be more important than the quality of the results.

  At worst, when this kind of program is established, it is usually by administrators and/or presiding judges who have no background or training in business litigation and do not understand that the techniques of ADR, which can be effective in resolving business disputes, are not the same as those used to resolve simple motor tort cases.

  At best, this technique, if presided over by a judge or attorney with a background or training in business litigation, can provide a valuable "Neutral Case Evaluation."

- *Mediation*: An experienced and thoughtful business conflict mediator, who is trained as a mediator and understands the unique nature of business disputes, recognizes that mediation is a process not an event.

  That means that the process of mediation in certain complex business disputes can take days, weeks, or even months and sometimes has to be staged. Information, which may not be known or even available when the mediation begins, may need to be exchanged or even developed. Disclosure of certain information, particularly information that may be arguably proprietary, might be both an internal and external issue.

  The trade-off between maintaining confidentiality for the tactical reasons, *i.e.*, reserving of information for litigation purposes and thereby reducing the possibility of settlement, may need to be explored by both counsel and client with a mediator facilitating the process. This is almost a sub-mediation within mediation.

  This is particularly true in intellectual property disputes where science may affect the value of the case. It is also a factor in cases involving financial losses where the nature of the market affects evaluation of damages. Specifically, where further scientific and/or economic analysis based on newly acquired information may well be ongoing as the mediation and the case progress as it might be essential to developing an accurate assessment of risk in order to determine the leverage that a party may have in the litigation and how that can change as time goes on.

- *Arbitration*: The challenge to this form of ADR, which is not often met these days, is to ensure that this process doesn't become a process that is just as lengthy and expensive as litigation. This can be difficult because accomplishing that goal, while at the same time ensuring that the process takes into account the special characteristics of business disputes, calls for the necessary balance between economy and efficiency and fairness. Fairness in these unique disputes requires the exchange of certain information, which should be considered to intelligently decide the merits of the case.

Chapter 21

When Is the Right Time to Negotiate?

"Woody Allen was wrong; 90% of life is showing up at the right time."

"When is the right time to negotiate?" is a question that is constantly being asked in every corner of the world from the local communities that we live in to the world stage, which provides the backdrop for the diplomacy and battlefields that will determine not only the quality of our daily lives, but in some cases our very continued existence. Illustrations abound all around us of the international, national, state, and local contexts in which this universal inquiry is repeatedly made and broadcast on the news 24/7.

The quality of our daily lives is affected by the answer to those inquiries in multiple ways ranging from the mundane and parochial—*i.e.*, will we have a National Football League season to enjoy this year to whether we will be able to live unthreatened in a "flattened world" with our "neighbors" in the Middle East and Africa in the aftermath of the "Arab Spring?"

Which of these issues is more important depends on whether the analyst is on the couch with a beer on a Sunday afternoon in the fall, or on the streets of Washington, D.C., or in an Arab capital this summer. The latest international context for the inquiry of "when is the right time to negotiate" to be propounded was broadcast in soap-opera style all last week. It began with President Barack Obama's speech on the Middle East, which was hyped in advance as his effort to "jumpstart" the renewal of negotiations between Israel and the Palestinians.

That speech preceded Israeli Prime Minister Benjamin Netanyahu's visit by 48 hours. The focus of the instant and arguably incorrect analysis of that speech's content regarding returning to Israel's pre-1967 borders as the "basis" for "renewed negotiations" offended Netanyahu, which resulted in a televised lecture and history lesson for the president of the United States on the virtues of recognizing historical realities as the basis for future Israeli-Palestinian peace negotiations.

It also raised the question of whether the right time to renew those negotiations was now or later after formal recognition and reconciliation of those historical realities, including the recent agreement between Hamas (which does not recognize Israel's right to exist) and Fatah to jointly govern and speak for the Palestinians in any future negotiations leading to the recognition of a Palestinian State.

The answer to the question of when is the right time to restart the Israeli-Palestinian peace talks will now be answered at a later date and will be more dependent on political factors and high-level personality clashes than it should be.

Nationally, we see the question of "when is the right time to negotiate?" being posed most often in the context of federal, state, and county governments trying to address a mounting "debt crisis." At the federal level, we hear ominous warnings from Treasury Secretary Timothy Geithner, and others, that we have to negotiate an increase in the statutory federal debt limit or face a "default," which has the potential to cause a financial crisis far worse than the one we are recovering from as well as the "catastrophic" result of destroying the world's confidence in our country's economy and with it our economic stability and credibility.

Weighing against this are both Republican and some Democrat political voices saying that the negotiations to raise the debt limit and prevent a default should not start until the Obama administration and congressional Democrats agree to negotiate both an increase in the debt limit and spending cuts, which are equal to the increase.

Democrats respond either by seeking to delink the issues of raising the debt limit from spending cuts or adding to the negotiations revenue-raising proposals at least in the form of eliminating certain corporate and special interest tax breaks.

In between childishly accusing each other of "exhibiting" or "lacking "courage," these elected officials are very simply being irresponsible and ignoring what clearly must be done. The time to negotiate a resolution of the debt limit and dealing with the federal debt crisis is now or before now. That obviously means that the debt limit, spending cuts, and revenue enhancers should all be on the table for discussion in these negotiations.

The people we elected "to do the right thing" should recognize as Michael Ignatieff, the former Harvard Political Science professor and contributing writer for *The New York Times*, now a member of Canada's Parliament and deputy leader of Canada's Liberal Party, has pointed out:

> *Good judgment in politics is messy; it means imperfect compromises that always leave someone unhappy—often yourself.*

Political theatre has visibly intruded on policy development as it so often does in our representative democracy. This is natural. But the staging of political theatre should not drive the timing of policy-making and its implementation.

Wise political leaders will not confuse the world as it is with the world as they, their handlers, and advisors might wish it to be. Nor will they assume their world view is presumptively correct and therefore should not be questioned in negotiations.

In other words, as former governor of New York and, as it turns out, prescient political philosopher, Eliot Spitzer, speaking on the subject of "The Need for Both Passion and Humanity in Politics," citing theologian Reinhold Niebuhr as his authority:

> *[D]riven by hubris, we become blind to our own fallibility and make terrible mistakes.*

Finally, right here in the state of Maryland and in the counties that we live, which are facing their own debt crises, we see high-profile, political decision-making by all three branches of state and local government. These decisions regard not only the compensation of public employees, but also their healthcare and their right through collective bargaining to have a say on those issues that directly affect the quality of their daily lives.

All over the country, in our state and recently in our own Montgomery County, Maryland, we have seen arbitrators' decisions favoring public employees and enforcing collective bargaining agreements set aside by judges on constitutional, charter, and statutory grounds.

These decisions bring into question the continued viability of the institutions and the integrity of the collective bargaining process, itself. They profoundly impact how and when future negotiations over the compensation and benefits of public employees at the state and local levels will take place.

It may well be those new governmental structures and processes, as well as the staffing of these functions with "Neutrals" whose intellect, integrity, and judgment are respected by both management and labor, may need to be designed to provide predictability and accountability for the negotiation of these issues.

Clear and stable lines of communication from workers to management, as well as structures and processes that ensure that results are final and not subject to politics or even budgetary economics, must be guaranteed in order to ensure that work confidence and morale is maintained and the quality of public services do not deteriorate.

The challenge at all levels of society and government as to how to determine when to negotiate is clear. We need to understand as did Dr. Aaron Miller, Fellow of the Princeton University Center for Scholars, in rejecting the conventional wisdom suggested by comedian Woody Allen, that "90% of life is just showing up."

Dr. Miller correctly noted:

> *Woody Allen was wrong; 90% of life is showing up at the right time.*

Chapter 22

ADR Is Here to Stay

"That is not an easy reality to accept for lawyers and law firms. It is, however, one to be reckoned with."

Norman Solovay, the chair of the Alternative Dispute Resolution (ADR) Practice Group at McLaughlin and Stern, LLP in New York, has pointed out:

> *Alternative Dispute Resolution or ADR is an umbrella term used to describe a panoply of techniques, some well-established, others emerging and evolving that can be used to resolve conflict without resort to litigation and without exposure to the increasingly unsupportable costs in time, money, and emotional stress that almost always accompany a protracted court battle.*

In an article in the September/October 2009 issue of *Business Law Today*, Solovay suggests that in the 30 years (20 years in Maryland) since ADR became an integral part of the lexicon of the practice of law and more recently the separate field of dispute resolution, it has been (and still is in many quarters) mostly seen at least by lawyers and judges as a "cross-practice."

This "cross-practice" is viewed by lawyers in mid-size to large law firms as something that can be utilized by the litigators in one or more practice groups and in certain cases, where to do so might be in the client's interest as determined by counsel.

When this determination is made, it is then and only then that a more focused discussion of exactly what is involved in these different ADR processes is undertaken to educate the client. That is unless the client has been previously driven by its own or industry economics to educate itself.

In many instances, as a result of that education, the company's lawyers come under pressure to minimize costs by providing ADR services or face the client's imminent departure to a boutique law firm or even an internally restructured client business model, which has in-house counsel providing the cost-effective dispute resolution services that their previous law firm did not.

The determination by counsel as to whether the use of ADR is in the client's interest in many instances is driven far more by law office economics, legal culture, and the personalities of the lawyers than any objective analysis on behalf of the client. If the decision is left to litigators, then it is likely that ADR will be utilized only when mandated by the court, by a contract dispute resolution clause, or to minimize potential losses and otherwise manage client expectations.

Ironically, the contract dispute resolution clause that requires mediation, arbitration, or both in many instances, may have been included by transactional attorneys in the same or similar law firms as the litigators who are grudgingly bound by them.

Notwithstanding that fact, mid-sized to large law firms' management committees, whose vision is limited to the short-term bottom line, have quite naturally pushed back against the spread of ADR, which appears to portend and may produce a direct hit against litigation revenues at least in the short term.

These management committees are instinctively supported by the litigators in the firm who became lawyer litigators because they liked litigating, as did this writer. I have been told by friends and colleagues—many of whom are highly accomplished both as litigators and negotiators—that they would "10 times rather litigate than mediate." The former is much more financially and professionally fulfilling. The latter is often draining and without glory, recognition, or reward as well as in most instances nowhere near the revenue generator that litigation is. The result is what Robert Margulies, a business litigator and mediator in New Jersey, called "Litigotiation."[2] That term accurately describes the pervasiveness of settlement negotiations in the litigation process.

What then would be the rationale for law firms to commit to a full integration of ADR into their practice? What promise does ADR hold in the new economic environment?

The most obvious economic answer is the competition between legal service providers that I described earlier. More than 98 percent of all cases filed are resolved before trial. But many of them settle only after long, grueling, and costly machinations, which exact a tremendous price on the client in time and money.

It is just this type of practice that all clients, but particularly business clients and their corporate counsel, seek to avoid. Furthermore, the evidence is that they will shift to lawyers and law firms willing to look at this larger picture and, if necessary, trade off substantial short-term litigation revenues for an approach that would better serve their clients if that is the only way to remedy their economic distress.

That is not an easy reality to accept for lawyers and law firms. It is, however, one to be reckoned with.

Once the decision has been made to fully integrate ADR into a law firm or practice initially, as I have said almost always for mostly long-term economic reasons, other and new issues will ultimately arise. Those issues will include ownership and management of cases as between practice groups and lawyers, choosing among alternative methods of dispute resolution and negotiation strategies and techniques, timing, bookkeeping, managing client expectations and rela-

---

[2] A term originally attributed to Marc Galanter, "Worlds of Deals: Using Negotiation to Teach About Legal Process," 34 J. LEGAL EDUC. 268, 268 (1984).

tions, development and training in new ADR skillsets, staffing issues, personnel, and technology.

These issues will have to be addressed not only for affected lawyers and law firms to be competitive in the legal services marketplace, but because the courts in all states, including Maryland, will no doubt at some point in the not-too-distant future follow the trend begun by the Chancery Court in Delaware and expand the inventory of dispute resolution services offered behind their multi-doors.

This will undoubtedly have the effect of putting a professional and economic premium on practitioners trained to provide them.

Older and Wiser

*"They should be cherished, defended, and reinforced
with all of their complexity intact."*

My first book, *Lessons Lived & Learned: My Life On and Off the Bench*, describes my journey through a public and private life, including memorable characters I have met, been mentored by, and experienced, along with the lessons learned from those individuals. Those persons include elected and appointed officials and political leaders, lawyers, and judges, as well as some colorful rogues and scoundrels.

Lessons Lived & Learned documents and explains my life's journey, the experiences and the people who guided me, detoured me, and made my stops and starts interesting—and at times, entertaining.

These "lessons learned" are presented in the context of a deep sense of humility developed over a period of time beginning in my ascendant teenage years, self-centered 20s, and even 30s and 40s when I was focused on climbing the perceived mountain of outward success and professional achievement that ultimately led to a successful law practice and three judgeships.

That road briefly descended in my 50s to a quietly disquieting personal valley of mid-life divorce and doubt for a short period of time. That time was comparatively brief, although it provided an intense learning experience that resulted in a much greater appreciation for the meaning of life, the value of the love of my children, grandchildren, friends, and family—even my ex-wife.

Later, in my 60s and now in my 70s, I am convinced that I am both older and wiser. Marc Freedman, chief executive at Encore.org and author of *How to Live Forever: The Enduring Power of Connecting the Generations*, documents the following conclusion:

> *There is a U-bend of happiness in life – on average, we're upbeat early on, then hit the skids in midlife before growing far happier later.*

That midlife skid is further explained by author and journalist Jonathan Rauch, who points out that in our 50s, we can see the deficiencies of the first half of life, but haven't figured out the second half's imperatives, even though as Stanford psychologist Laura Carstensen explains, we realize that there are fewer years ahead than behind. This realization drives us to seek deeper connections than what we had previously with those we care about.

This book follows my first book for a very specific reason. In this book, I hope the older and wiser Steven Platt has been able to relate the lessons of his life's journey with the two big "Hs"—humility and humor.

The Australian-born writer, Clive James, wrote:

> *A sense of humor is just common-sense dancing. Those who lack humor are without judgment and should be trusted with nothing.*

I agree!

Most of the columns, blogs, and speeches in this book are about the people, institutions, relationships, commitments, and trust that I and others have relied on during our lifetimes. Particularly now, many of them appear to be failing and under attack.

They should be cherished, defended, and reinforced with all of their complexity intact. Arthur Brooks, president of The American Enterprise Institute and author of *Love Your Enemies: How Decent People Can Save America from the Culture of Contempt*, acknowledges that our problem in America is not as widely believed—incivility or intolerance.

Rather, it is as explained in a 2014 article in *The Proceedings of the National Academy of Sciences*, "Motive Attribution Asymmetry," the "assumption that your ideology is based in love and your opponent's is based on hate." The researchers found that today, the average Republican and the average Democrat suffer from a level of "motive attribution asymmetry" that is comparable with that of Palestinians and Israelis. That is, each side thinks it is driven by benevolence, while the other is evil and motivated by hatred, and is therefore an enemy with whom one cannot negotiate or compromise.

These positions are taken by people who have lost their sense of humor and any semblance of humility—or never had them to begin with. They need to either get them back or be replaced by people whose personal transformation has evolved to the extent that they can lead the necessary social transformation.

That evolution, to a certain extent, as *New York Times* columnist David Brooks points out, is a product of age—the stage of life when one has reached his or her 60s and is mature enough to recognize that contempt is, in the words of philosopher Arthur Schopenhauer, "the unsullied conviction of worthlessness of another" and is "a noxious brew of anger and disgust."

I believe this book reflects that I am both older and wiser. If that means my words can help rescue our relationships and institutions, my purpose will have been served.

Other Books by This Author

Black Robe Fever

The Role of the Judge in American Society

Of Politics & Economics

The School of Hard Knocks and Gentle Persuasion

Lessons Lived & Learned

My Life On and Off the Bench

RAMSES HOUSE PUBLISHING LLC
BALTIMORE, MD

Index

P

R

S